ETHNOGRAPHY
LESSONS

ETHNOGRAPHY LESSONS

LESSONS

A PRIMER

Harry F. Wolcott

Left Coast Press Inc.

Walnut Creek, California

Left Coast Press is committed to preserving ancient forests and natural resources. We elected to print this title on 30% post consumer recycled paper, processed chlorine free. As a result, for this printing, we have saved:

2 Trees (40' tall and 6-8" diameter)
1 Million BTUs of Total Energy
206 Pounds of Greenhouse Gases
992 Gallons of Wastewater
60 Pounds of Solid Waste

Left Coast Press made this paper choice because our printer, Thomson-Shore, Inc., is a member of Green Press Initiative, a nonprofit program dedicated to supporting authors, publishers, and suppliers in their efforts to reduce their use of fiber obtained from endangered forests.

For more information, visit www.greenpressinitiative.org

Environmental impact estimates were made using the Environmental Defense Paper Calculator. For more information visit: www.papercalculator.org.

LEFT COAST PRESS, INC.
1630 North Main Street, #400
Walnut Creek, CA 94596
http://www.LCoastPress.com

ISBN 978-1-59874-580-1 hardcover
ISBN 978-1-59874-581-8 paperback

Library of Congress Cataloging-in-Publication Data

Wolcott, Harry F., 1929–
    Ethnography lessons : a primer / Harry F. Wolcott.
        p. cm.
    Includes bibliographical references and index.
    ISBN 978-1-59874-580-1 (hardcover : alk. paper) —
    ISBN 978-1-59874-581-8 (pbk. : alk. paper)
1. Ethnology—Fieldwork. 2. Ethnology—Authorship.
3. Ethnology—Qualitative research. I. Title.
    GN346.W66 2010
    301—dc22
                            2010030798

Printed in the United States of America

⊗™ The paper used in this publication meets the minimum requirements of American National Standard for Information Sciences—Permanence of Paper for Printed Library Materials, ANSI/NISO Z39.48–1992.

CONTENTS

INTRODUCTION

A "primer" (*prim'er*), I am informed by my trusty dictionary (American Heritage, fourth edition) is, among other
things, "a book that covers the basic elements of a subject,"
not to be confused with *pri'mer,* "an undercoat of paint or
size applied to prepare a surface, as for painting." This is
a *prim'er* intended to cover some of the basic elements of
ethnography. It does not provide an undercoat intended
to cover *all* the basic elements—there are other books for
doing that. They do it quite well. (I immodestly include
Ethnography: A Way of Seeing among them, but it is *a* way
of seeing, not *the* way.)

No, this book is intended for those who have become
serious about ethnography and would like to know just
a bit more before actually engaging in it. And since you
can't yet share your experiences with ethnography, I have
set out here to share mine. Old-timers among ethnographers will no doubt agree with some of the points I make
and will disagree with others, but they have to accept that
this is the actual course of events and the evolution of my
studies and that these are the lessons I have gleaned from
them. I have not assumed, however, that you necessarily
are familiar with any of my written accounts, and I have
tried to say enough about each of them as they are introduced so that you understand what prompted the lesson.

As an ethnographer, I look back on these forty plus
years with satisfaction, although *my* experience with

ethnography no doubt fails to put me among a class of swashbuckling adventurers. I guess you could place me among most academics whose adventures are generally of a sort that must be judged by the depth of their studies rather than the danger of their missions.

I have constructed the text around my five major studies, all of which have been reported in published texts, beginning with my dissertation study among the Kwakiutl Indians of British Columbia and ending (almost literally) with a book called *Sneaky Kid and Its Aftermath*. With all five texts in place it has been easy for me now to move among them, and it may surprise you to find that I begin with a key lesson from my *second* study, *The Man in the Principal's Office: An Ethnography*. The reason for that, as you are about to learn, is that is where these lessons actually began to sink in.

What follows from there is a discussion of some critical components of ethnography often mentioned but seldom written about: the subjects of serendipity and personal ethics, for example. I also want to share with you the results of my career-long search for the essence of ethnography. So on the one hand, the book promises to tell you a lot about ethnography without guaranteeing that you will learn anything new except about how I went about it, and on the other hand, if it is all new to you, I hope you will find the lessons sufficiently informative that you will want to learn more about ethnography before, or as, you try it for yourself.

For myself, in a lifetime of ethnography, I could not have found a pleasanter way to live a productive life and feel the satisfaction of doing something worthwhile. And I found that I *always* had something to write about. I hope you find or have already found your own satisfaction in beginning to pursue ethnography.

And now, let the lessons begin ...

CHAPTER ONE
Ethnography Lesson

The chapter that I am about to deconstruct was originally written in the period 1968–1972, so its story is hardly newsworthy. In its final version this chapter originally appeared in 1974 and proved to be a great success. It remained in print for years. I have taken this opportunity to share the lessons I learned with other beginning ethnographers. I have written about this material before (Wolcott 2003c), but in that writing I erroneously laid my problem to a problem with writing, rather than to my lack of understanding about ethnography.

What seems most curious is how I happened to save the earliest draft of that original chapter and the subsequent critiques to it that I received. My file drawers have always bulged, a particular problem for any professor who remains at the same institution for so long. Of course, my office moved from place to place and building to building as education experienced its incessant but cosmetic changes. However, the moves were never so dramatic that I needed virtually to chuck everything in order to make the shift. At one time my small office contained five file cabinets full of precious (to me) documents. Still, I was constantly throwing out old material. I suspect that I kept *this* set of comments with the intention to write more about it someday. Now, more than forty years later, I am able to fess up.

The story has multiple strands, but it all began with meeting George Spindler, professor of education and anthropology at Stanford University, in 1960 when I embarked on a course of doctoral studies. I was unaware that such a program existed until I met Spindler. I realized that a program combining anthropology and education was the kind of program that interested me, even if, as I suspected at the time, it didn't necessarily lead anywhere or at least to a position that anyone was trying to fill. Those of us who elected to study with Spindler were simply willing to take our chances, perhaps hoping later to apply for a position probably in some department of social foundations of education.

With Spindler's direction, coupled with a large dose of serendipity (to be discussed in chapter 3), I went to Kwakiutl country on Canada's West Coast to do dissertation research. By the time I completed my fieldwork and had written my dissertation in 1964, there was some call for students of education who had included anthropology in their studies. I took a position with a new educational research center at the University of Oregon, the Center for the Advanced Study of Educational Administration. The center was one of a number of new federally funded educational research and development (R&D) centers established under President Lyndon Johnson's plan for developing the Great Society. I have been at the University of Oregon ever since.

For my initial assignment at Oregon I was seconded to a sociologist to assist with a normative study of school administrators, not much of an assignment for an anthropologist, but I was too junior to be set free with a project of my own. At Spindler's urging, I eventually proposed a new assignment more to my liking, studying what one elementary school principal did in the course of his daily work. Of course, studying what a principal does did not seem like terribly exciting stuff. I would have preferred to study a classroom or even a whole school. But my interests were constrained by the mission of our research center; I needed to put an administrative spin on the project to win approval.

What I proposed was to follow one school principal around "in anthropological fashion" to see what he (little question in those pre-affirmative action days that it would be a "he") actually did, in contrast to a literature that was essentially hortatory in nature, reporting what a good principal should or ought to do. This was a natural assignment for me. Immediately prior to attending Stanford, I had been the vice principal of a huge elementary school. I also held a California administrative credential. I would be studying something in which I was already well informed.

During my early years at the Center (1964–1966), I managed to rewrite my dissertation for publication as *A Kwakiutl Village and School* (Wolcott 1967) for the new series in Education and Culture edited by my mentor. That substantially increased my status as an anthropologist in the Center and attested to the fact that I could "do" ethnography. And Spindler seemed to like what I had to say in that study, at least after he was able to get me to go beyond my data to say what I thought it all meant. That was a not-so-easy jump in those days when we were trying hard to substantiate our claim as empirical observers.

By the end of the academic year in 1966 I had located a school principal willing to allow me to conduct my proposed study, and I began making visits to his school as often as three or four times a week. Although I had projected a study of one year for the fieldwork and a second year to write it up—not an unrealistic projection, I thought, since that is how long my Kwakiutl study had taken—I found that with teaching responsibilities and other university obligations, I needed to continue my fieldwork for a second year.

During this time I was becoming aware of how the field of anthropology and education was burgeoning. Suddenly there was interest aplenty in ethnographic research, and positions were becoming available for applicants with appropriate anthropological training.

Meanwhile, Professor Spindler had enjoyed good success with his recently edited book *Education and Culture: Anthropological Approaches* (Spindler 1963) and had decided to prepare a second edition. He was even considering preparing a totally new book instead of simply revising the old one. And that put him on the prowl for possible new contributors. As one of his students, I was among them.

With an eye to promoting his already well-received series, the Case Studies in Cultural Anthropology, Spindler contacted the authors of that original set of monographs to see if they had anything to contribute to his new volume. Since he had always shown an interest in my projects, he asked if I had something to offer from each of my studies, the Kwakiutl study and now the school principal study. But he laid down one condition: he did not want articles warmed over from those case studies, he wanted new material that would complement what we had already written as well as attract new readers for his book. He posed the question to me in an interesting way. He knew I was then beginning to write up my fieldwork, so he asked, "Is there anything you might share with others who may be having trouble with drafts of their own?"

Agreeing to write the piece was not an easy decision. True, I realized that I was expected to get an article or two from my study, and the invitation from my former Ph.D. adviser meant that he would reserve a place for me in his forthcoming book. My problem was that I had completed the fieldwork for what would was destined to become *The Man in the Principal's Office*, but I had not yet written one word of it. Shouldn't I work on the full study first, rather than spin off a piece for someone else's edited collection? Then again, an article for Spindler would have a guaranteed publisher and a ready-made audience. I opted in favor of the sure thing, rationalizing that the writing would not take long (!) and would buy me time to complete the full account and find a publisher.

The pressure to publish has not diminished during the ensuing years. But unlike most of my colleagues, my appointment as research associate allowed time to pursue research as my major activity. Although I held an academic appointment, it required only part-time teaching. I had now completed two years of funded research, and it was time to show what I had accomplished. Further, from day one my study had been touted as "ethnography," a book-length ethnography at that. My colleagues wondered just what an educational ethnography looked like, especially a study conducted in a local elementary school, rather than on some remote and exotic island.

Without having written the full study, however, I did not know what I should include or exclude. I did not see how to describe in an article-length piece what I would eventually spell out in detail in my book. Spindler imposed no control over content except that he wanted the article to complement my as yet unwritten book—to be an original piece rather than an excerpt.

Because of that experience, I have always counseled others to write their full and complete account first, if there is to be such an account. The advice seems reasonable; one ought to know if a story is to be told both en toto and piecemeal. The decision is not quite so straightforward, however, and as must already be apparent, I did not follow my own advice.

Where to Begin

I was ready to write about the principalship. I did not intend to write about how I had gone about gathering the data, a "method" that seemed rather mundane to me. But there was much interest in how I had conducted the study and what made it "ethnographic"—and not a few skeptics who wondered if there really was any "method" to my work at all. So method had to be there, at least enough to satisfy an audience of educators that here was a different way to conduct research. If I was going to talk about method, I needed as well to lay out my purposes and how ethnography was going to help me achieve them. I began my draft for the forthcoming Spindler chapter with the following vignette:

> The following dialogue occurred while a special committee of school principals was interviewing candidates for new principalship positions which were to be filled the following year. The candidate being interviewed was a principal from a nearby rural district.
>
> > *Interviewing Principal No. 1:* "Why do you say you like autonomy?"
> >
> > *Candidate:* "I like to be an individual, just like you do."
> >
> > *Interviewing Principal No. 2:* "Do you like your teachers to be individuals, too?"

Candidate: "Yes. As a matter of fact, I encourage it."

During a period of two years, May 1966 to May 1968, I tagged along with one elementary school principal to study what it is that principals do, how they feel about it, and how the many other roles they play as human beings affect and are affected by their role as principal. To my amazement, I have occasionally been asked, "Did the principal know you were making the study?" I can assure you that he did, as did his faculty and family, all of his fellow principals, many visitors to the school, and even quite a few of the pupils. A few of the pupils even learned the nickname which the faculty assigned to me as a way of jokingly acknowledging what I was about: "The Shadow."[1]

That first draft ran to thirty-eight pages. Three pages of introduction were followed by seven pages describing my ethnographic approach, eleven pages discussing "salient aspects" of the principalship, and a conclusion discussing paradoxes in the role. I wrote comparatively, across the role, rather than confining my observations only to the case study principal.

I prepared the draft during the summer, mailed it off to Spindler in August 1968, and received his comments two months later. I felt pretty well into ethnography at that point. My first book, transforming my dissertation into one of the original volumes of the new *Case Studies in Education and Culture* series edited by the Spindlers had been published the previous year. Now, the fieldwork for my second study was completed, and I had begun to write it up. My brilliant career.

Spindler did not usually edit on a point-by-point basis, but he peppered my draft with comments. I guess I kept copies of the evolving manuscript all these years to keep me humble. His words were never unkind, but they went right to the core of the problem—and to my core, as well. No doubt Spindler recognized the importance, or the *potential* importance, of this effort of one of his early students to make the case for educational ethnography. He wanted me to say it just right. If I couldn't say it by myself, he would say it with me. If necessary, he would even say it for me.

On page one of my draft he offered a critical examination of my discussion about method:[2]

* Pp. 1–12. A little meandering. Needs sharper focus—exposition and defense of why as well as how you study only one man and his operational context.

* How do you justify studying *one* principal in order to understand principals?

* Questions to answer in 1st part: What did you want to find out? Why do you call it an *ethnography*? Why couldn't you find out other ways?

Further along, where I sing the praises of capturing dialogue but fail to employ any, Spindler asks, "Yes, but what use is the dialogue? Dialogue is good to use, but its relevance should also become clear." I also introduced and defended the idea of viewing the principal's behavior in cultural terms. Spindler's note on that point was succinct: "Too vague. What are cultural terms?"

By page 5, Spindler seemed to be getting nervous: "After a brief Introduction, with more observational materials, the paper could start here." [I still find something similar on every early draft I circulate. It reminds us all to look again at beginnings: first sentence, first paragraph, first section, entire first chapters. Realize that it may take *us* a while to warm up, but while we're at it, our readers may be cooling out. We need to get right at it, the quicker the better. It doesn't hurt to attempt to snag your reader by stating your purpose with your opening sentence.]

Once through method, and twelve pages into the manuscript, I did (finally) launch into what principals actually do. I explained my purpose: "I have chosen to make some rather broad statements, and I have chosen to speak about the elementary school principalship in general rather than restrict my comments to the actions of one man over a given period of time." Were I given to using a lot of italicized words in my writing, every word in that sentence would now be italicized, for they reveal the essence of my problem.

In the margin, Spindler raised a profound question with a simple word: "*Why?*"

He pointed out that I could make the case that this principal was like all others in ways that could be defined through other kinds of studies. And he recognized that I did observe other principals in the course of my study. But he reminded me that my study was about *one particular principal.* From the outset I had jumped the track. I was keeping my observational data largely to myself, using them only as a springboard for reviewing the principalship in general.

By page 31, Spindler had seen enough generalizations. He started changing my every use of the word "they" to "he" to try to get me back on track. But reading half a page later he gave up on that approach and issued a directive in the margin: "Don't generalize. The heart of ethnography is singularity." Where I had written "Most principals organize their time in such a way that they minimize unencumbered time or eliminate it completely," he responded in the margin, "Show this in *this* case."

I did eventually get down to cases. I wrote about a series of meetings in which "my" principal and five other principals were convened as a screening committee to make recommendations about who among many candidates looked promising for positions that would open up the following year. But even here, rather than restrict my comments to the deliberations at hand, I could not resist going to the literature to review studies from California and New York for perspective on the phenomenon I was examining,

I decided to send Spindler this new draft as a work-in-progress to get his reaction, for even I had begun to feel that my words were getting nowhere. I was, as Gertrude Stein once described it, trying to say everything about everything, to fit everything together and squeeze it all into one draft. Instead of writing the article Spindler had requested, I had begun writing the book. To do that, I had to transcend what I had observed about my principal's behavior in order to talk about the principalship.

I hoped for encouragement and support. I didn't get a lot of it, but Spindler was always patient. On the back of this copy, I found some positive comments under the heading "What's Good." For this topic he listed five points:

- direct observation and anecdotes
- limited to one situation that can be studied *thoroughly*
- extraction of themes (but *how* did you?)
- the indecisions about role and leadership [He marked this with a double "+."]
- brief exploration of procedures stressing multiple research activities, intimate observation, closeness to subjects, repetition of experience in different settings, etc.

I was relieved to see that he found some good points. As I look at that page now, however, I'm not so sure these were points he actually found, as much as points that he hoped to find, threads he hoped to see developed. And although the category "What's Good" appeared at the top of the page, I suspect it was an afterthought, a way of letting me down gently. In bolder writing, his main message is contained in the following points, listed as "Suggestions" for developing the draft:

1. The methodology and Introduction per se should be disposed of in no more than 6 pp.

2. The substance of what you found should be presented inductively, with substantial behavioral slices, and excerpts from oral interchanges, then interpreted briefly. The gist and value of your study is its intimate view of *one man* in a known context, but the text does not at present convey this, like Roger Barker's *One Boy's Day*.[3] You will be hit hard for overgeneralizing.

3. You give the impression of trying to generalize to *principals*. This is not your purpose. An ethnographer never generalizes to other cases. One might, in interpretation, compare *specific* other cases, or hypothesize about the broader scope of phenomena.

To put it bluntly, *I wasn't writing ethnography!* I didn't have to wait to be "hit hard," Spindler himself was punching me out, if only figuratively. My study was mired in a sea of words about principals, my every observation reported as a generalization pertaining to all principals rather than tracking the behavior of the one I had observed so meticulously for so long. Writing was not my problem. My problem was my misconception of ethnography.

I was dumbfounded! Eight years of working with Spindler, including a successfully completed dissertation that had been turned into a book, yet apparently I did not really understand what it meant to make a study "ethnographic." There was no question that I had lots to say about principals. But the whole point of ethnography was not sufficiently clear that I recognized or even trusted it. Why indeed study just one person?

I tried to figure out what had made my earlier study about a Kwakiutl village and school a success, and where the present study was going awry. Then I realized: the Kwakiutl study was already bounded for me. I was situated in a tiny village community of thirteen households on an island along the coast of British Columbia. I was the teacher in a one-room school. I was the only resident White, with little chance during the year even to get to town (Alert Bay) or to visit other villages. All I knew about, and thus all I could write about, were the students in my class, their parents, and other villagers. I could not generalize about the Kwakiutl in other villages. Nor could I make comparisons with the past; everything seemed so different from the traditional literature on the Kwakiutl and my circumstances in 1962–63.

It is not that I finally produced so splendid an ethnography of the Kwakiutl. My colleague (also a student of Spindler) Ronald Rohner, conducting his ethnographic study of a neighboring village during the same period, described my efforts at the village part of my study as "solid and competent" but likened it to reading a "catalogue of observable culture traits" (Rohner 1968:654). Although Rohner's praise for the village part of the study was faint, he judged the school portion of the monograph as "insightful and dramatic." And no wonder. That was the part of the story that I lived and breathed. It was the part I really understood.

With the principal account, however, I knew a great deal before I initiated the study. As noted, I had been a public school teacher, having served four years in two California school systems before going to Stanford to work on a doctorate. I had a master's degree in school administration. I had served for a year as vice-principal of a large elementary school and had even been approached about assuming a principalship for the coming year. I probably could have written this account without setting foot in another elementary school. One reviewer unkindly suggested that I might have done just that. He did not accuse me of it, he merely found everything I wrote so "obvious" that he noted I *could* have done so. He probably would have liked what I was writing now. He showed little patience for the level of ethnographic detail that Spindler wanted to see.

And that was the difference! Although I could base my principal study on observed behavior, I knew—and had far more to say—about the principalship than that.

There is nothing wrong with that approach. The literature on school administration is filled with such articles, written either by former principals or by students of educational administration. But an *ethnography*, my mentor was now patiently trying to get me to understand, was antidote to existing practice. "What specifically did *your* principal do?" he kept repeating in his comments in the margins: "Don't tell us about them all. Tell us about the *one* you have been observing for the past two years!"

What Spindler was calling for was retooling, and on a grand scale. Initially, I held to the course I had set, rewriting and tinkering with word order. By December I had another draft, still holding fast to ideas I had been trying to develop. My rationale must have been that my problem was nothing more than a writing problem, that Spindler would come around if I just got the words right. I began circulating my draft among colleagues. The copy I have of the next version clearly shows its links with the earlier one.

The Ethnography Lesson

Finally, it struck me! What Spindler wanted for his new book would require a completely different approach, some *part* of the story told in depth rather than a preview of the whole study. I simply couldn't get there from here. It would take a total rewrite, with a clear focus on some particular event or series of events for illustration.

I did have an incident in mind that I could use, the one from which I took the opening vignette of my original draft. But now I had to make a choice: put that account in Spindler's book or save it for my book? Then I realized that I could draw upon those meetings (three in all) in which "my" principal had been appointed to the ad hoc committee to screen candidates. I had already wondered whether to introduce the story of those meetings in my account, but in the book it would have been necessary to identify him among the interviewers. Examining the proceedings of the committee *as a committee* would allow me to make some observations without having to identify my principal. I would not have to single him out; he could still make his appearance as an individual in my book. I could base my story for Spindler on the proceedings of the committee as a whole, a story within a story.

I arbitrarily assigned the group a formal title: the Principal Selection Committee. With a focus on the actual dialogue of principals and candidates, I could produce the kind of specificity that Spindler was calling for, and I could illustrate aspects of the principalship through specific examples.

Make no mistake, the observer-researcher always has a perspective, always offers a point of view. What to add, and how much, is a major aspect in the art of writing up fieldwork. Our accounts would be sterile indeed if we reported nothing more than observed behavior. What I needed to recognize was how much, and of what, an ethnographer might add in such circumstances. My early drafts were typical of what educational researchers were writing—those few, such as Robert Dreeben (1968) and Phil Jackson (1968) who actually ventured into the field. I would have to add something more to my observations to make ethnography of them.

I wasn't just honing my skills as an ethnographer, I was beginning to learn how an ethnographer looks at a study like mine. Granted, it was a particular kind of ethnography—what today goes by the label of a "person-centered" approach. Richard Fox describes it as attending to "the everyday life of persons, not the cultural life of a people" (Fox 1991:12). The approach suited me fine, even if it was a bit embarrassing to be discovering what ethnography was about so far along in my career.

Although not all my subsequent research has been "person centered," my studies have always focused on *one* of something studied in depth: one village, one individual, one institution, one effort at change.[4] And they are studies of everyday life, not of culture. I realized that "culture" is the biggest generalization of all, a concept useful for keeping the anthropologist oriented but of no utility in presenting data. Find the particular, and draw upon it to establish some broader themes that cover more cases and begin to form patterns. Not history, but a kind of natural history. As I looked for ways to tighten the article for Spindler, I realized that identifying some recurrent themes would provide a way to summarize and make sense of elements of the study. Otherwise I would have nothing more than a collection of seemingly haphazard remarks from members of the selection committee and responses from their interviewees.

Searching for Cultural Themes

In my earlier drafts I had identified three tentative themes: (1) money, (2) status, and (3) goodness, the latter dealing with the idea that principals strived to be "good," almost too good to be believable. [That was forty years ago; I think principals still like to be perceived as decent men and women, although I am not sure they are as compulsive about it these days or feel that it gets them all that much.] With a fresh start, I could now throw out my three themes, or at least be on the lookout for more powerful replacements. I was at the point where tossing out everything seemed the quickest way to get going again.

However, Spindler was keenly interested in my section reviewing method. I found a toe-hold there. But the main thrust of the article would be the events of the selection committee, beginning with a description of the candidate interviews.

Now that I was in a "singular" frame of mind, there seemed to be both too many interviewers and too many interviewees to keep track of. Among the principals, "my" principal's participation was not especially noteworthy. I decided to make the comments and questions anonymous, giving the five principals a collective voice rather than trying to sort them out individually, since each of them had an opportunity to ask only one or two questions during the brief interviews, and the questions seemed not to lead anywhere. One principal had served on a similar committee the previous year. On that occasion they had agreed on a uniform set of questions to ask each candidate. This year they decided just to let the interviews "happen."

At most there were only four anticipated position openings in the coming year, so there were also too many candidates—fourteen of them—and not much information about some of them. The committee decided not to interview them all. They pared the number to interview to no more than eight candidates. For my purposes, I didn't need even that many. When the proceedings were over, I decided to present a few candidates in the order in which they were finally ranked and to use their rank order name rather than assign pseudonyms. The top ranked interviewee became Mr. First.

I still remember being impressed with how great a range of age and experience was represented by the original pool of candidates. There were male and female applicants, from within and outside the school district, ages thirty-one to sixty-one, experience in education from eight to thirty-nine years. All had master's degrees, all were experienced elementary school teachers. I was even more surprised to realize at the conclusion of the proceedings how the selection committee winnowed out the variability to give their highest marks to a set of finalists that were virtually carbon copies of themselves, except they were a few years younger. The committee had dealt with the variability by eliminating it—and a major theme for my article had evolved.

Identifying "themes" was clearly my responsibility, something that I added to the descriptive account to push it beyond simply selecting principals. I was not satisfied with the three themes I had identified earlier (e.g., money, status, and goodness), yet new ones did not seem to emerge.

I shared my developing draft with a member of the anthropology department, Alfred G. Smith, a linguist who was quite taken with the notion of general systems theory. From his perspective, he noted how the principals seemed to engage in what he called "variety reducing" behavior, as opposed to the variety-generating behavior suggested by a job description of the principal as instructional leader of a school. I pondered his idea, not only as an apt description for the results of the committee's deliberations but for much of the behavior I had observed throughout the fieldwork. The principal and his colleagues all talked change and innovation, but they worked essentially at containment, holding the system together in the face of the multitude of forces for change that swept around them. They hardly needed to foster change in such a setting.[5]

That idea worked well for interpreting the study. It was the result of serendipity—all that I provided was a receptive mind and a recognition of the goodness of fit between observed behavior and an idea floating around in one social scientist's head. Had I asked someone else to review the manuscript, perhaps a different theme would have evolved. It is not that principals are variety reducers by nature, but that variety-reducing describes a great deal of their professional behavior. Labels, like styles, come and go. It has always seemed a shame to me that the terms "variety reducing" and "variety generating" behavior have never found a more prominent place, at least in the literature of educational administration.

Many months later, when I finished the longer study, I concluded it with a final quote that seemed at once to sum up and impose the biggest restraint on the principalship,

"Every problem is important." But I hadn't gotten that far at the time of writing the piece for Spindler. I posited more cautiously about the lack of professional knowledge associated with the role. It was difficult to identify something that was not there, but I could point to the absence of both a technical language and a specialized body of knowledge. That was why I was personally taken with the opening vignette I had originally selected, about a principal who not only claimed to "like autonomy" but believed that he "encouraged it." Yet that comment, too, had to be deleted. It required too much explaining to make the point without seeming to make it at the expense of a candidate—and of the proceedings themselves.

My third new theme concerned "Esteem for personal feelings." It complements the point described above—that in the absence of professional discourse, esteem for personal feelings seemed to take precedence. In the selection committee meetings—and in every situation in which I observed principals—personal courtesy was in abundant supply and personal feelings were part of every assessment. Of one candidate, for example, a committee member remarked, "A member of my staff said he [the candidate] walked right by her the other day without speaking. She felt badly about it. Of course, that doesn't pertain here." But, of course, it did. The only thing that trumped the feelings of others was the feelings of members of the selection committee themselves. For example, of another candidate one interviewer remarked, "I feel some reservations about how he relates to kids. But there's no question of his ability."

I learned something about themes in the process of identifying a few for my study. Spindler asked pointedly where I got them. At first I took that to mean that they ought to spring right from the data, their links so apparent that all the ethnographer has to do is uncover them. I think what Spindler was suggesting was only that I should note the origins of possible themes in the specific actions that suggested them. Like culture itself, cultural themes must be "attributed," and it is the ethnographer who does the attributing. Themes are (or were in an earlier day) an important way to begin to map out a culture. I am not sure we can do without themes if we want to do cultural analysis today, although, like culture itself, the idea of cultural analysis may seem somewhat passé.

Something observed must prompt the themes proposed; they don't just grow out of thin air, nor are they handed down from on high. Were ethnographers not able to reach some level of generalization, we would be doomed forever to report nothing but the details of behavior, plodding stuff indeed. My theme-making had to be ratcheted down a notch or two to have some basis in observed behavior. Over time, I assumed, the better themes would survive and would account for more observed behavior; weaker themes would disappear or be subsumed. There could be many themes or a few. My proclivity for threes probably accounts for how I happened to settle on three themes. The theme of variety reducing behavior seemed to account for more behavior than the other two, so I saved it for last, to suggest that here was a theme that described a great deal of the managerial behavior of (many? most? all?) principals.

Rewriting the Account

My article also needed a stronger beginning. The opening vignette I had employed amused me but was unlikely to make sense to other readers. I subsequently found a short entry I made one morning after a meeting of the Principal

Selection Committee. Committee members decided to have lunch together before returning to their respective schools, and I was invited to join them (Dutch treat, of course). We were seated in a local restaurant when some of my university colleagues happened by. Recognizing the group of principals, one of them commented, "Harry, you ought to watch the company you keep." To which the principal of my study promptly quipped, "He does!" referring, of course, to my role as ever-present ethnographer. A splendid way to begin the article and get right to describing what I was doing and how I was going about it.

Refocusing my article did not go quickly. It took six months before I had a new draft to show Spindler. He seemed delighted with the new focus on the Principal Selection Committee. He also felt that my identification of the three themes held up well. But he expressed concern about how I had summarized the ethnographer's task, reminding me that the way I had conducted my study was not the only way such studies can be done (and wincing, perhaps, because I had drawn on an article by sociologist Morris Zelditch [1962] in summarizing my work as a "field study"). He took pen in hand to restate more forcefully how an ethnographic approach allowed me to study one principal. And once again he changed my plural conception of principals to the singular: *one* elementary school principal.

Spindler wanted me to explain how the principal was enmeshed in a cultural system. He proposed an extension to the paragraph I had written:

> These roles, and the interaction of the people filling them, are the human elements of a cultural system, the school system of one community, that is the context of the principal's behavior, and of this study. To the extent that the cultural system involved in this study is similar

to other cultural systems serving the same purpose, this ethnography of a single principal should produce knowledge relevant to the understanding of such roles and cultural systems in general.

Imagine my surprise to find these very words, unattributed in my published piece, almost exactly as Spindler scribbled them in the margin of my manuscript forty years ago. I could see why he wanted to press the point of what we can learn from a single case. Apparently he felt that I had not given it sufficient emphasis. So I added his words to mine, not quite certain what they meant but quite certain that they should be included.

By May 1969 I had a final draft that satisfied us both. Spindler wrote, "It is, of course, clear as a bell and just fine." He also noted that he was considering a different title for his book, now planning to rename it *Education and Cultural Process: Toward an Anthropology of Education.* He was getting so much new material that he felt the book should be new, not just a rehash of *Education and Culture.*

I was now free to turn attention to my intended book, preparation of which had been delayed almost a year. We anticipated that the copyediting on Spindler's new book would be done in 1970, with publication in 1971. But 1971 came and went, as did 1972. Spindler kept announcing "last call," and I dutifully kept making minor changes, but the manuscript was essentially finished. By 1972, I also had a final draft of *The Man in the Principal's Office.* The book was published in 1973, a year ahead of the shorter piece I had prepared for Spindler.

By then it was I who was getting after Spindler for the delays. But he was working on an *edited* collection, and he could not speed up production unless he simply dropped wayward contributors. His vision for the book was compelling. He was also involved in other writing projects, and he had plans to write several new chapters of his own in addition to reprinting some chapters that had originally appeared in *Education and Culture.* I was trapped in other people's writing schedules, something one can never foresee and cannot remedy (unless one withdraws an invited manuscript written specifically for a text).

It is hard to imagine, though, how my final study would have turned out had Spindler not intervened with an invitation to prepare a separate article for his book. I know my account would have been far less "ethnographic." I believed I had a lot of general information about principals that the world would find interesting. I felt an urgency to rise above my case study material rather than get bogged down in it.

When the moment finally arrived, I asked Spindler if he would be willing to review the draft of my completed book about the princpalship. He was sufficiently impressed with it that he wanted it for the Education and Culture series, which since 1967 had grown to a remarkable sixteen titles. But after reading the book, he expressed disappointment that my account seemed more like a sociological role study than an ethnography. He could find evidence in support of that conclusion in my use of such terms as *socialization* rather than *enculturation,* the notion of *sponsorship* for a role, and the important reference to my work as a *field study* rather than as *fieldwork.*[6] To disabuse him of the notion that my book had a more sociological slant, I boldly added the subtitle, "An Ethnography." I felt that readers could at least be informed of my intent (see Wolcott 1987). I also resolved to make my studies even more "anthropological" in the future—now that I finally understood how to go about it.

I am pleased with the ethnographic research and writing I have completed since that experience, measured not only by a reasonable output through the years but also by the number of things I have written that have been reprinted or translated. Although it took six years to get published, the chapter I discuss here has remained in print ever since, the most recent of its five reprintings in 1998, thirty years after I began work on it (see Creswell 1998). I take pride in the accomplishment in spite of the rocky road I had to travel to get there and my initial lack of appreciation for what ethnography can best accomplish.

CHAPTER TWO
Minding The Ethnography Lesson

Quantitative researchers often confess to "mining" their data, referring to going through data again and again to see if there is anything of interest that they might have missed in earlier efforts to comb through it. I don't sense that qualitative researchers follow a similar practice. Their work with data tends to be cumulative. But as the preceding chapter relates a personal experience of ethnography, I feel that I should reflect on some points that may have been passed over too quickly or, because of their importance, not emphasized sufficiently. So let me sift back through the account to both "mine" and "mind" the lesson(s) of the previous chapter in order to emphasize some subtle points that warrant more careful attention.

What Can You Learn from Studying Only ONE of Something?

One of the most insistent problems of the principal study arises around the issue of why bother to study only *one* of anything? What can be learned from studying only one member in a group? And how do we know if the one we happen to have chosen is representative?

I found an answer in something Margaret Mead wrote

years ago. I am not sure that it is the complete answer, but it is at least part of it. I quote Mead for those without easy access to this chapter in Kroeber's authoritative text of 1953. She here is discussing what she calls *anthropological sampling*, something that occurs whenever an anthropologist builds a case on the basis of only one or a few known instances:

> Anthropological sampling ... *is simply a different kind of sampling,* in which the validity of the sample depends not so much upon the number of cases as upon the proper specification of the informant in terms of a large number of variables.... . Within this very extensive degree of specification, each informant is studied as a perfect example, an organic representation of his complete cultural experience. [Margaret Mead 1953:654–655]

Mead states that this kind of sampling came about historically to explain how anthropologists are able to describe a society when only a few survivors of a broken or vanished culture remain. This is similar to the work of the linguist who can discern the grammatical structure of a language with a single informant (but needs several informants to see the *patterns* of language use). What I take it to mean is that one needs only to be able to specify an informant's *place* or *status* within a group.

To illustrate, the principal in my study was a married Protestant male in his forties, who had been a principal for a number of years after teaching in the elementary grades for several years. He was a career principal, not someone intent on becoming a superintendent. On each of these variables he was "typical" or "like most other principals" in the huge national sample. To reiterate Mead's words, he was, therefore, "a perfect example, an organic representation of his complete cultural experience." Of course he did not represent everyone in the principalship, but he was typical to the extent he exhibited these common characteristics. More on that later.

How Much to Say About Method?

How much needs to be said about method? You probably are more aware about method than I felt I needed to be in the 1960s when ethnography was first catching on in education. The biggest mistake one can make today is to present as a discussion of method a broad and detailed history of some central technique (e.g., participant observation, interviewing) yet fail to describe the *specific* methods employed for capturing the data actually used in the write up. The reader does not want to hear about the development of efforts to validate the idea of participant observation or of your personal problems, such as how long you went without mail or how you were tormented by mosquitoes; the reader does need to know specifically how you gathered the information that you used in order to assess the extent that what you have to say can be relied on. Did you depend mostly on one or two informants, for example, or did your information come from a broadly distributed group? We must not lose track of the fact that our readers want to evaluate our reporting, just as we have tried to assess the group or individuals about whom we write. I have always suspected that anthropologists have an undue capacity for making generalizations (they have to be in order to answer the kinds of questions they get asked), and I suspect that they do the same in the field. So, from how many perspectives did you get your accounts of important events that occurred?

As fieldworkers, we also need to specify *ourselves*, in the same spirit that Mead asks us to specify our informants—with enough detail that we, too, can become organic representatives of our complete cultural experience. Our readers have a right to know about us. And they do not want to know whether we played in the high school band. They want to know what prompts our interest in the topics we investigate, to whom we are reporting, and what we personally stand to gain from our study. I have recently tried to test the limits as to what researchers can reveal about themselves (see Wolcott 2010).

Boundedness

There is nothing wrong with boundedness in a study; it is an essential quality that sets limits on what we can handle. The parameters of a study define its boundedness. Among the Kwakiutl I had no problem with boundedness; the limits of what I could write about were provided by the island circumstances of the village. There were no comparable limits in the principal study—there were principals at every level, from the local school district and state to a national organization. I could hardly contain myself. That is why I was so eager to say something about *all* principals, even to the point of totally bypassing my case study principal. Therein lay my problem.

Spindler brought me back to earth with my "ethnography lesson" and helped me understand that all studies are bounded, and the broader their boundaries, the less use we can make of them to understand what is happening "on the ground." If I were beginning the principal study today, I would bind it even more closely to the behavior of the *man* in the principal's office, and without apology, for that might better acknowledge the limitations of my study but also fulfill its potential. I did include one chapter titled "The Principal as a Person," but that was only a nod to the fact that he was a man who happened to be a principal rather than a principal who happened to be a man.

Getting and Acknowledging the Help of Others

Our studies, like our lives, are overdetermined, the result of the many and diverse influences on our behavior. I have found that it doesn't hurt to be as explicit as one can be about those influences and to offer appreciation and acknowledgment of that fact along the way. The idea that a book or article is solely the creation of its author is patently absurd. So my chapter for Spindler acknowledged the early help I received, and my book acknowledges an even wider spectrum, including people who helped with particular chapters, as well as others like Spindler who had already exerted a major influence on my career

Every account has a story behind it. Make that two stories, the public one that may be at least partially revealed, both in the writing and in the acknowledgments, and a private one that may remain totally beneath the surface. There may be more even to this lesson about ethnography than I have disclosed, for I am limited now to what is contained in an old file folder and to memory, and the memory part is compromised by the years since *Notes from a Field Study* was first drafted. (For example, I cannot imagine that I was not a bit annoyed with Spindler's consistent rejection of my original idea for the chapter.) I recognized early on that without the evidence of Spindler's comments I might conveniently have forgotten that I wrote the original draft without the least appreciation of what this ethnography might, and should, look like.

By 1968, I was becoming skilled at moving words about, and it took a long time to realize that my underlying problem was a conceptual one, not simply how to put a paragraph together. We don't need to hear every story about the secret lives of manuscripts, but some good might come out of more disclosure among active writers as to the kind of help they asked for and the problems they faced. Such stories will be most helpful as they relate truthfully everything that happened along the way to exert a subtle—and sometimes not so subtle—influence on the finished product. Such stories might also include discussions of articles that never make it to print, for reasons not always germane to their content.

One's choice of outside readers is obviously critical. I pass along an idea gleaned from the study of culture acquisition, an idea posed long ago by anthropologist Sol Tax. Tax once mused, although I am not aware that he developed the idea, that age-grading is far more important among humans than we recognize. He pointed out that we learn a great deal (did he say "most"?) of what we know from those at about the same age or just a bit older than ourselves, just as we exert our most important influence on those the same age or a bit younger (Tax 1973:50). In terms of sharing drafts of academic papers, I translate Tax's idea to sharing a manuscript with someone a bit ahead *academically* of where we would like to be.

That is why Spindler was an ideal critic for me. He was hitting his prime as a masterful editor and author, while I was just getting started (there is a difference of exactly nine years between us; we celebrate the same birthday). Whether I was obliged to incorporate his words exactly as written may seem questionable, but he was struggling with ways to make ethnography useful, especially to educators, while my concern was with how to make my study "ethnographic enough." I afforded him some space to do it. After all, it was his book.

Nevertheless, any time I receive a draft back from an invited reviewer, I face the agonizing decision of whether or not to make the recommended changes, especially those requiring major reorganization. Reviewers have their own style and agenda; they may confuse where I am heading with where they wish I would go.

But I seldom have been as far off the mark as with the paper described in the previous chapter, in which I confused the *work* of the ethnographer with the *authority* of the ethnographer. Based on two years of fieldwork, I felt that I had established my authoritative role. My patient mentor had to disabuse me of that idea and get me to turn attention to the remarkable mountain of data that I had accumulated but was poised to ignore. Yet he, too, had an agenda. His concern was with the development of the field of anthropology and education and how ethnography was represented as its research tool. I had to ignore his concern that my study appeared to be so sociological; I was just beginning to see how to get any anthropology at all into such familiar settings.

Themes

One doesn't hear enough about themes these days, at least in what most anthropologists are writing (but see Bernard and Ryan 2010:53–73, for an exception). That strikes me as a shame. The themes I identified in the principal study, especially the theme of variety-reducing behavior, seemed to offer a good way to encapsulate the essence of the principalship. Themes are ways to put patterns of behavior together to get at the heart of the matter, and that is the *ethos* of a culture.

I was impressed with the concept of themes when I first heard about it, and I am still inclined to think in those terms—something that makes grander use of the patterns that we observe in repeated but minute observations of behavior. The risk in using them is that you don't know if you really have properly identified them, and the best way to prevent that problem is long-term fieldwork where you have time to generate possible themes and time to check them through continuing observations. The work of anthropologist Morris Opler is cited as an early source of discussion and example of the use of themes (Opler 1945; 1964).

The precursor to finding themes is to identify patterns of behavior, and the precursor to that are the minute observations of specific instances of behavior—the little vignettes that we enter into our daily field notes. But there is no reason not to be thinking "themes" from the beginning of your study and trying to test your early hunches, and even less reason not to discard those that do not seem to pass muster.

Assigning Pseudonyms

You will notice that I was able to avoid using pseudonyms in the article about the principals by simply giving rank order names to applicants. That proved a very workable resolution, but I was not clever enough to make it my standard practice. In the full account I employed some pseudonyms that served me adequately but failed to amuse teachers at the school. Mrs. Duchess was not delighted with her pseudonym, nor was Mrs. Skirmish. I might have kept those names for my personal amusement until the final draft without doing any harm, for they served to help me to keep track of the numerous roles that people played, but it was not necessary to make them public. I could have substituted the grades the teachers taught; that would have been the least confusing.

I learned how unsettling pseudonyms can be when a reviewer, expressing his disdain for what something I had written, dubbed me "Wally Haircut" throughout his offensive review (Roth 2005). A comparable mistake on my part was to assign the name "Sneaky Kid" to the lad who came to live on my property some years later. The name stemmed from his own account, when he explained that was what his mother called him when he got into a cake she had meant to keep for an evening desert, but it also created the image of an immature youth rather than the streetwise young adult that I encountered. The lesson I have learned is to avoid assigning *any* pseudonyms (or altered names) if at all possible, and certainly not to clutter up a manuscript with names that do not serve the purpose of helping readers keep track of who is who.

Implicit in this advice is also the caution to be careful in assigning each name, title, or subtitle to your work. I called my first book by its appropriate descriptive title, but the name *Kwakiutl* presents a hazard for unwary readers. The end result was that readers unfamiliar with the name often mispronounced it, misread it in some humorous way, or simply avoided it. What a book does not need is a title that others cannot pronounce, or characters whose names cannot be pronounced. But I still had not learned my lesson. In my study of African beer gardens I confused my readers with another name, the city of Bulawayo where the research took place, the pronunciation of which I myself remain uncertain to this day.

Graphics

Since publication of the first edition of their book, *Qualitative Data Analysis,* in 1984, Matt Miles and Michael Huberman have urged qualitative researchers to "think display." But for me, their important message seems to have been constantly diminishing.

I was asked to include a map of the region of Vancouver Island for the initial publication of *A Kwakiutl Village and School,* but the map drawn for me was poorly made and had to be redrawn for subsequent publication. At the time *Man in the Principal's Office* was ready to be printed, publishers had grown wary of lawsuits and they did not want pictures of the real school, with or without people present. Even an accurate map had to be turned on its side, with the misleading name of a main boulevard in another Oregon city affixed, so the school could not be located. The publisher of *The African Beer Gardens of Bulawayo* was happy to include photos that I supplied, as well as several provided for me that were strictly for promotional purposes, and, after all, Africa is a long ways away. It did not seem wise to include any photos from the disruptive case of *Teachers Vs. Technocrats.* The only photos that remained for the publication of Sneaky Kid were of the cabin as it stands today.

I have obviously been remiss in failing to "think display" as often as possible and at least to have included more maps among my publications. Yet I have been critical of professional publications that definitely needed a map (see, for example, Wolcott 2001) and have expressed disappointment in any reading where a text cries out for more maps or more detailed ones (e.g., in non-fiction accounts such as Greg Mortenson and David Relin's *Three Cups of Tea*).

Time

There will never seem to be enough of it. The best way to manage time may be to work diligently only at things that are of deep and genuine interest to you, so that you never feel that you are wasting whatever time you have ... and if you had even more time, you assure yourself, you could accomplish even more. I can think of nothing worse than working on a project that had no interest for me, but keep your spirits up, that may be where serendipity can play a hand—the lesson to be discussed next.

A further comment on time. Fieldwork takes time, writing it up takes longer than expected, and arriving at a satisfactory conclusion of what it all means may seem to take forever. You simply cannot rush the process! Say what you can say by way of summary but do not necessarily consider your work finished. It may take several years for you to figure out just how things fit together, and then you may be ready to write again or to add to your earlier statement. To illustrate: I finished my dissertation in 1964 and had a slightly improved ending by 1967, but it was not until 1989, some twenty-five years later, that I felt I finally wrote the conclusion I hoped someday to write (Wolcott 1989). And as I mentioned at the beginning of chapter 1, I have already reworked the material of that chapter in an article published in 2003, yet it finally occurred to me that I had mislaid the cause of my problem to *writing* rather than to my *misunderstanding* of what ethnography was about. You can't rush your conclusions—just be patient. Probably better to treat them as "interim conclusions," to allow for better ones that may someday follow.[1]

CHAPTER THREE
The Role of Serendipity in Ethnography

In chapter 1 you saw a remarkable example of *serendipity* in action, in a fortuitous event that definitely saved my article and probably saved my career. The lesson of this chapter is to unveil some of the serendipitous events in my life so you can be on the lookout for how this seldom addressed aspect of fieldwork may play a part in yours as well.

Serendipity

As you can guess from this writing (some remarkably old references coupled with a few new ones), I am at an age now when I spend more time looking back over what I have accomplished than looking for what to do next. It has been a good career, and I am satisfied enough with it, but I have at times felt more satisfaction than seems warranted, as though I alone did it, and I did it all alone. That has created a new concern.

It might be more appropriate to think of myself as serendipity's child, an eager and grateful recipient of its blessings. Serendipity is a nice word—it slips easily off the tongue and is usually morphed simply as fortuitous "luck." But cultural anthropologists employ it in a special way when talking about fieldwork and the opportunities that arise for them in doing that work. For them the term suggests more than just luck, it implies good fortune and even, as my trusty dictionary informs me, a certain aptitude for making desirable discoveries by accident.

The dictionary even gives a short history of the word. It credits English author Horace Walpole with coining the term from an old name for Sri Lanka, today's modern Ceylon, as part of the title of a silly fairy tale describing the travels of three princes of Serendip who were always making discoveries by accident of things they were not searching for.

Something similar happens for the ethnographer, a person who makes it his or her business to learn about how others usually go about their daily lives. There has to be a healthy dose of serendipity operating in order to learn what one is trying to understand, since there is no obvious starting place or sequence for relating such accounts.

One can examine the life cycle from birth to death, or use a list of standard categories employed by anthropologists such as Social Control, Social Organization, Economic Organization, World View, and so forth, or describe the life history of a particular person or provide an abbreviated version of the story of some group, but without serendipity during fieldwork (or some lucky breakthrough during the subsequent writing) the final report is likely to be sterile and uninteresting. With serendipity working for you, you make discoveries and uncover patterns—some by accident, others with a gentle push—but you are always poised to *make the most of whatever opportunities happen to come your way.*

How Serendipity Has Worked for Me

So I would like to tell you how I think serendipity has enhanced my life. I will examine some of the serendipitous events that played a role, both professionally and personally, and thus have contributed to my sense of accomplishment. In short, it is a confession of how events over which I had little or no control have had a major part in my life as a fieldworker, including a few lucky choices that I made among the options that presented themselves. Opportunities, if you will, but sometimes with little idea where they might someday lead.

I attended UC Berkeley as an undergraduate. That sounds impressive, but it wasn't. My family lived in Oakland at the time, and I went to Cal because it was so close to where we lived that I could get there by streetcar. Most of my high school classmates attended there as well. And the tuition wasn't too steep—about $26 a semester, as I recall—a whopping $52 a year. I don't even remember that the question of where I would go to college ever came up in my home. Both my parents attended Cal, although, as was standard in those days, my father went directly from high school to UC Dental School in San Francisco, and my mother never completed her studies.

As for my part, I felt that I received a terrible education there. By the time I graduated, I hated school so much that I vowed never to set foot in another classroom. Nor was there much choice or discussion about being drafted into the army after graduating. I was whisked into military service, but I was never sent overseas. That was due not to my powers of persuasion or because I was a graduate from Cal, but because I had elected to take one elective class—*typing*—in high school. Typing skills were always in short supply, so once I received my permanent assignment (to Fort Lewis, Washington) I remained there until my participation in the war was no longer needed.[1]

Change of Heart

When I got out of the army I reflected on my life to that point, and, with the GI Bill in support, I decided to give education one more chance. The GI Bill was my first real encounter with serendipity (unless you count not being sent into a war zone as the first). A whole new world opened for me at San Francisco State College. In spite of my earlier resistance to the idea, I thought I might enjoy and be successful at teaching. With encouragement that I had not experienced at Cal, I thoroughly enjoyed my year of preparation at San Francisco State, and since I already had my bachelor's degree, a year of additional coursework was all I needed to be certified as a public school teacher.

Following that, I taught in Richmond, California, as an intern teacher for one year, and in Carmel, California (a happy coincidence in itself), where I received tenure, for the next three. By that time, serendipity had begun to play a serious role. I received an invitation from Stanford University to study for a Ph.D. That was based on some good grades and some great teachers I met at San Francisco State (like Aubrey Haan), so grades and professors finally did matter, no thanks to Berkeley!

At that time doctoral students in education at Stanford were encouraged to take advantage of the wider course offerings in the social sciences, rather than feel they had to limit themselves to the study of education. Fortunately for me (you can see serendipity at work again) anthropology was among the approved subjects, and there was a young professor there named George Spindler, an anthropologist with a particular interest in cultural transmission.

I elected to study with him and to pursue coursework in education and anthropology, which then required a formal Ph.D. minor in cultural anthropology.

There really was no "field" of anthropology and education at the time, but the combination seemed fascinating, viewing educational processes in cultural perspective. That meant looking at education broadly conceived, rather than only at what is taught in schools. In other words, looking at the process of *enculturation*—how we become the social human adults we are to become rather than looking only at what we are supposed to learn in school. I was hooked, although it was not clear what any of us could do with the degree when we completed the program. At the time, there were only two university positions in anthropology and education in the United States. And my mentor occupied one of them.

But by the time I completed my doctorate in 1964, interest in anthropology and education had grown. For a brief period, more attention was being given to the role of the social sciences in education than there had ever been. And because of that, my first appointment was the only one I ever sought. I was appointed to the faculty at the University of Oregon, with a posting to its new R&D Center.

By then, serendipity really started to kick in. The original push at Oregon had been to find an anthropologist interested in studying aspects of formal education. But all the university's anthropologists were occupied doing their own thing, as usual, so there was neither interest nor support from the anthropology department. The search had to be expanded to try to find someone in the field of education who was also trained in anthropology. Voila! Guess who just happened to have the right credentials?

Some of my Stanford professors felt it was a bit short-sighted to take a position on the West Coast and remain relatively close to home, but I went to Oregon because the university was looking for someone with anthropological training. I have been at Oregon ever since.

Just how much of an anthropologist was I? Well, serendipity had already played a major hand in where I did my fieldwork, and fieldwork has always been identified as the *sine qua non* for the cultural anthropologist. In discussing my proposed dissertation with Professor Spindler, and with his help, I planned to take a teaching job which he had arranged on the Hobbema Indian Reserve in Alberta, Canada, to do a study of Indian education. Indian education at the time seemed to be pretty much of a bust. I visited Alberta to scout the school where I would probably be assigned.

But next came a moment when serendipity seemed about to elude me. Spindler's contact person in the Indian Affairs Branch in Canada was suddenly transferred from Alberta to British Columbia; he no longer was in charge of staffing Indian Schools in Alberta. He could only offer to assign me to an Indian Reserve somewhere in British Columbia, if that would be okay. My new assignment was to a one-teacher school in a Kwakiutl village.

If you are familiar with the history of anthropology in the United States, you realize that the Kwakiutl people play an eminent role. Not because they are unusually interesting (which they are to me) or because their masks are more beautiful, their customs stranger, or their traditions more spectacular than those of other First Nations peoples, but because Franz Boas, who is often called the father of American anthropology, did a great deal of his fieldwork and writing based on his continuing work among the Kwakiutl.[2] One of his earliest students, Ruth Benedict, practically immortalized the Kwakiutl in her popular book *Patterns of Culture*, written in 1934 but still widely read. It was my very good fortune to do fieldwork among the Kwakiutl.

In my completed dissertation, I observed and reported from two perspectives: first, the school and village from the villager's point of view, and second, from that of a White village teacher (me). I subsequently was invited to revise my dissertation for publication as *A Kwakiutl Village and School,* published in 1967, in a new series in education and culture edited by my mentor and his wife, anthropologist Louise Spindler.

I am pleased to report today, more than forty years after its initial publication, that book remains in print. It lacks the beauty and grace of Ruth Benedict's *Patterns of Culture*, but its anthropology is not as dated. And to whatever extent a book can do so, it validated me as an ethnographer/anthropologist. Although finishing the book (de-dissertationizing my account, as I have referred to it) took three more years, the fact that I had successfully done fieldwork validated my claim as ethnographer. And in securing a job teaching on a Canadian Indian Reserve, it certainly didn't hurt that I was an experienced classroom teacher. Things were beginning to fall into place.

A New Beginning

Ph.D. in hand, I arrived at the University of Oregon as a research associate, ready to put my anthropological knowledge and experience to work. Although the idea of having an anthropologist on the staff was appealing for the image the Center wished to build as a multi-disciplinary endeavor, no one there had any idea of what an anthropologist did in that role. Including me. My immediate thoughts were about rewriting my dissertation, but I had to do that on my own time.

I was seconded to a sociologist for a couple of years while I thought about how to energize my role as an educational anthropologist in a Center whose mission was the study of educational administration! The mission presented a new problem—coupling the Center's objective to make its work relevant for educational administrators and my need to make it relevant for an anthropologist.

As I have explained, Spindler understood my plight and suggested that I might study one elementary classroom, treating it as a little community and getting to know each individual pupil and the teacher and the parents so well that I could say something about the classroom as a "small society." Yet that possibility seemed a pipe dream, not really workable in terms of obtaining necessary permissions, nor immediately relevant to educational administration.

To fit the circumstances at hand, a seemingly better alternative was to look at a school by studying what a principal does, compared, say, with a village chief. *One* school and *one* principal, studied over an extended period of time—that seemed feasible enough, and potentially anthropological enough. The idea won the support of the Center's administration, and I was finally on my way. I initiated a proposal for a year-long project of sustained fieldwork in one school, followed by a couple of years to write it up—assuming that I would still carry out other responsibilities, such as building a new course sequence in the now recognized field of anthropology and education.

I searched for a local principal willing and sufficiently interested to allow me to conduct the study in his school. The study is the one you read about in chapter 1. As noted,

I was often asked, "Did the principal know he was being studied?" He most certainly did, and he remained comfortable with my constant presence. He even started bragging about his participation in the study, and I had to caution that if my study was going to be informative, it would be more than the testimonial he hoped for.

I also anticipated criticism from other researchers. In studying one principal, how would I know if he was representative of his group? Good fortune was with me again, for during the year of my study, the National Association of Elementary School Principals conducted a huge nationwide survey, and my principal fit in the middle range on every variable imaginable (gender, age, religion, marital status, etc.). Besides that, I had Margaret Mead's reassurance that an anthropologist *should always be ready to defend the study of a single case (!)*, that each informant is a perfect example, what she called an "organic representation of his or her unique and complete cultural experience" (Mead 1953).

Although I have never claimed that my principal was typical, I know that in most respects he was representative of many individuals in that status. [I should add that I have never met anyone, in any role or occupation, willing to claim that he or she is "typical."]

First Sabbatical

That study completed and almost under wraps, it was time for a university sabbatical, the practice of freeing up college faculty every seventh year to further their own studies or research. My partner Norman and I eagerly anticipated the sabbatical leave, but I had no idea of what to do or where to go other than to add to my fieldwork repertoire. I knew that I did not want to conduct a study of another principal, and I had begun to think that what I needed was something more exotic and definitely more "anthropological" (i.e., cross cultural). Certainly more dramatic than driving across town to my research site in a local school. I applied for a Fulbright Scholarship, but nothing came of it. I felt stumped.

Then a former student from the university (Dr. Donald K. Smith, founder of DayStar, Inc.) asked if I would be interested in spending a year in southern Africa, where I might teach his missionary colleagues something about applied anthropology but would otherwise be free to pursue research on my own. Serendipity had beckoned; I jumped at the opportunity. Airfare to Southern Rhodesia was paid for me, and Don Smith helped us settle in Bulawayo, Rhodesia's second city, where he was conducting missionary work. [Southern Rhodesia, as I am sure you know, is today known as Zimbabwe.]

In the early 1970s, Rhodesia was an exciting place to be, but it was not especially dangerous or beset with the terrible problems it was yet to face. It was then White dominated and independent, and the idea of studying in an "African" (i.e., Black) school seemed inviting and appropriately cross-cultural. Meanwhile, Norman found a teaching job in a private residential school and also became actively involved with local theatre.

But I could not get into the schools—even in those days, no one in charge was very excited with the idea of having an American anthropologist snooping around. I found myself in Rhodesia and the anticipation of a year with no idea of what to do.

I took the opportunity of a free "public relations" tour into the African townships adjacent to the White community, a segregated area where all Blacks who worked in the city were required to live. The tour included a brief visit to see one of its many beer gardens.

In Rhodesia, as throughout southern Africa, the beer gardens were, at the time, operated by local municipalities for their African residents. It was a money-making endeavor, supplying inexpensive "African beer," brewed locally. The main function of the beer gardens seemed to be to help the native population remain contented with their lot.

[I should note that African beer is nothing like our clear beer brewed with hops. It is brewed from fermented cornmeal and is low in alcohol content. It is thick and a bit sour, if you can imagine drinking a bowl of cool, thick Cream of Wheat. It is served in huge plastic mugs which are usually shared among a group of drinkers. Try as I might, and I did try, I could not develop a taste for it.]

During my stay in 1971–72, the city of Bulawayo produced and marketed an astonishing *fifteen million* gallons of African beer a year! The profits were used in part to provide amenities for the African population, including social workers whose task was to shore up some of the problems caused by making beer so inexpensive and readily available. That struck me as a bit circular. I thought it would make an interesting study, especially for readers back home. But if I couldn't even get into the schools, it seemed extremely doubtful to me that I would be allowed in the beer gardens, which were operated strictly for the African population.

It was worth a try, however, so I made an inquiry to Bulawayo's Department of Housing and Amenities, those responsible for making and brewing the beer and operating the beer gardens, about conducting a study.

Serendipity had to be working for me. I was told that the man in charge, "The Chief," as subordinates in his department referred to him, happened to be away on holiday. My research idea was given *provisional* clearance, pending his return. The Chief turned out to be Hugh Ashton, who, I was to learn later, happened to be an anthropologist and who, some years earlier, had done fieldwork and published on the Basuto people of South Africa (Ashton 1952). He was now head of Bulawayo's Housing and Amenities Department. Among his various responsibilities, his department supervised the local making and selling of African beer.

When The Chief returned, I immediately made an appointment to meet with him and try to win approval for my project. To my utter surprise, he totally embraced the idea of my doing a study. He seemed quite interested in it. But then he added some provisos to his affirmation:

> If you just want to have a *look around,* you are welcome to do so. But if you expect us to provide you with *office space,* and if you expect us to provide you with *research assistants* to help with translation [local natives spoke two non-intercommunicating dialects of the Bantu language, Shona and Ndebele], and if you expect us to help with *transportation,* and if you expect us to help with *getting materials typed and mimeographed,* then ... [he paused, and I thought "here it comes"] we would at least ask you to provide us with *a copy of your report.*

That was all he asked! I was dumbfounded. The lesson is that if you ever envision a study that you would like to do, there is no reason to believe that you will not be allowed to do it until you ask. (And I hope you will find the likes of a Hugh Ashton when and if you do.)

I had most of the year to conduct research, and I devoted full time to it. Rough as it was, I had a working draft that I could present before I was ready to return home. And Ashton was as good as his word, even providing me two assistants, one Shona-speaking, the second a speaker of Ndebele, to assist with my beer garden interviews. Just before I left Bulawayo, Dr. Ashton had copies made of my draft report, and together with his entire staff we went through it sentence by sentence, not with the intent of censorship but to see that I had my facts right. Whenever there was any doubt, all he said was, "You may want to check on that."

My experience in Africa clinched the point that I was a capable ethnographer, and serendipity smiled on the whole proceeding, in spite of the fact that it was an entirely unplanned adventure. For example one day, upon returning to our apartment, Norman asked, "Would you like to interview some Africans whose medical problems are a result of their drinking?" Of course I would, I answered, but how would I ever make contact with them? "Well," Norman replied, "I just discovered that one of the board members of the theatre group I am helping is a psychiatrist who works with those people everyday. He says he would be happy to arrange a visit for you."

In fieldwork, as in life, one thing leads to another, and my interest in beer gardens turned at one point to the nutritional value and medical consequences of beer drinking among residents of the African townships. It takes a lot of thick African beer to get drunk—one is far more apt to feel full before feeling any effect—but some people devoted almost full time to the effort and, second only to trauma caused by beer garden fights, there was a curious phenomenon sometimes associated with drinking to excess, called iron overload or, locally, Bantu siderosis.

In looking into this problem I had already joined doctors at Mpilo, the local African hospital, donning the same white coat that hospital staff wore (and allowing myself to be called doctor, which, technically, I am), but my curiosity was piqued about the nutritional value of the beer as well as by the siderosis problem, and my newly acquired medical colleagues suggested that I should meet with the head of the medical school in Rhodesia's capital city, Salisbury (today renamed Harare).

Some time later I had occasion to travel to Salisbury, to attend an academic seminar on the campus of the University College of Rhodesia. I fully intended to meet with the head of the medical school while I was there. But once I actually arrived, I lost my nerve—who was I to be making an inquiry that to him would undoubtedly seem more like the inquiry of a snooping American journalist than an anthropologist inquiring into facets of a fascinating and complex social problem? I chickened out on my resolve to interview, or even try to arrange a meeting with, the dean of the medical school.

On Friday afternoon, midway through the conference, I grew weary of listening to presentations, and I decided to return to my hotel in town. There was no public transportation on the campus, but I knew that I could make a long walk out to a thoroughfare where a local bus stopped, even if I was unable hitch a ride. So I thumbed, as I hiked along the road to the bus stop, surprised that so few cars seemed to be leaving campus in the late afternoon. And those that did were not stopping to give me a lift.

Finally one car did stop. The driver asked where I was headed. It was in the direction he was going—and I hopped in. He was interested in what an American was doing in Rhodesia; in turn, I asked what he did on campus.

And guess who the driver of the car turned out to be—none other than kindly Dr. Fraser-Ross, dean of the Medical School, the one person in the whole world I most wanted to meet at the time! Talk about serendipity!! I explained the coincidence to him and briefly described my project. In turn, he not only drove me to my hotel but insisted that I join him and his wife that evening for dinner. We carried on a correspondence for the rest of that year and for several years after. His help was invaluable on medical matters and on current research into drinking-related medical problems of urban Africans.

After that, serendipity seemed to know no bounds. I completed an early draft of my study the following spring, and finished editing it after I arrived home. The book was subsequently published by the Rutgers Center of Alcohol Studies in 1974, complete with an enthusiastic forward prepared by ... Hugh Ashton.

My experience in Rhodesia also came with another unexpected lesson. If I was genuinely interested in anthropology *and* education, I realized that I had veered off course in looking so whole-heartedly into the cultural traditions of urban Africans. In my effort to validate myself as an ethnographer I had thrown myself completely into the role of the cultural anthropologist. I found a way back to my own field by looking at how young people *become* beer drinkers, what one has to learn to "pull it off" in knowing what kind of drinker to be, just as we, too, learn the appropriate drinking or non-drinking behaviors appropriate for our gender and for each of the social groups in which we participate. So my book, *The African Beer Gardens of Bulawayo,* contains a section devoted to "Becoming a Drinker."

I returned to the States ready to resume my role as research associate in the R&D Center. I resolved to try to make, or to keep, the anthropological contribution more apparent in my studies of anthropology and education.

Return of the Native

In my absence, the mission at the R&D Center where I held my appointment had changed. Its focus was no longer simply to *do research* in schools, but to do things to *dramatically change* schools, presumably for the better. Educators have always insisted that everybody knows what goes on in schools, so time was no longer to be devoted to understanding schools better or examining how one goes about making *effective* changes in them. There did not seem to be any need for an anthropologist. The scene didn't augur well for my intended goal of bringing more anthropology into the study of education.

I was still part of the research staff, however, and the director of the R&D Center looked for a project where I might make a contribution. He found it in one of the Center's ongoing projects, one attempting to implement an adaptation of PPBS for school practice. PPBS had grown out of fascination with <u>P</u>rogram <u>P</u>lanning and <u>B</u>udgeting <u>S</u>ystems (thus PPBS) then the rage in government circles. The project at the Center included an adaptation of PPBS being developed for, and now being demonstrated and implemented in, the schools of a nearby community.

All the director had for evidence of the effectiveness of the project, however, were glowing reports from the developers themselves about how the project was progressing. Would I prepare an independent report, perhaps for his eyes only, on what was really happening?

At first, I didn't see much opportunity for anthropology in the assignment; it was more like becoming the project's historian, or worse, the director's private detective. But I quickly discovered that the program was causing HUGE problems in the school district where it was being implemented, partly because of the picayune nature of the program itself ("Mickey Mouse in triplicate," as one teacher put it), and partly because of the way the implementation effort had proceeded to jam the project down teachers' throats. Resistance had reached a point where the teachers had organized a district-wide committee to hear grievances and examine the problems the program seemed to be causing. As an anthropologist assigned to look into the situation, I would be a supposedly impartial observer.

Second Sabbatical

Time for another sabbatical—this one to Malaysia, where my friend Robert Gaw headed the International School in Kuala Lumpur, and where Norman took a one-year teaching assignment. I found an opportunity to observe a community development project in action (Wolcott 1983b).

Then back to the States, where I was teaching full time while the research center was gradually being phased out. And here came an opportunity that seemed a diversion at first, a request from a publisher to prepare a monograph on the topic of writing for the Sage Series on Qualitative Research.

I will never know exactly how publisher Mitch Allen identified me as someone who might write about writing, but when he asked if I would be interested in doing such a book, my immediate thought was that I should give it a try. That writing assignment put me forever in a writing frame of mind, and as Gloria Steinem has observed, "Writing is the only thing that ... when I'm doing it, I don't feel that I should be doing something else."

The little monograph that resulted, titled *Writing Up Qualitative Research,* has now seen two revisions, and apparently has helped many students get their research written. Its success prompted Mitch to ask, "What are you going to do for us next?" I can't think of anything better to spur one to keep on keeping on than a question like that. And now I could call more of the shots in defining what I wrote about. As I have grown older and less flexible, less anxious to go out and "mix with the natives" for months at a time, I have kept busy without having to rely quite so heavily on serendipity.

More recently I have turned attention toward writing about doing ethnography and to the art of fieldwork. These are hardly "starter" topics for a beginning ethnographer; far better, I think, to begin writing with something more immediate and more concrete, and take it from there.

Lesson Review: Serendipity

Fieldworkers often toss off the fact that it takes a lot of time and a lot of luck to make a go of fieldwork. However, this is luck of a sort one can have a hand in; serendipity suggests that you make the most of whatever opportunities confront you rather than worry that opportunities will never come. As I will show in chapter 6, sometimes that requires one to turn an unfortunate circumstance completely on its head, and to rethink or restructure the original course one had set.

I have tried to show the important role that serendipity has played in my fieldwork, beginning as far back as the GI Bill that allowed me to return to school in spite of the fact that my first opportunity was so negative. That began a series of events that I now look on as exceedingly lucky, although in some cases I made a choice or at least made a positive interpretation of what was happening.

Studying with George Spindler at Stanford proved to be fortuitous, and doing fieldwork among the Kwakiutl was a decided plus among younger anthropology colleagues. The support I received from the village chief and others in the community was exceptional, and even now, forty-five years later, I remain in touch with some villagers.

There were also opportunities that I had to forego at the time. For example, the village chief expressed interest in relating his own life story. Had I elected to follow that route after my year at the village, I might have joined the small group of anthropologists who have become authorities on contemporary Kwakiutl culture. (But note a cautionary message here, you may be confronted with more opportunities than you can handle. To whatever extent you are able to control your own destiny, do not get distracted by projects that are not relevant for where you intend to go.)

If there was any serendipity operating at the time of my return to the Stanford area after fieldwork to write my dissertation, it was in the wonderful place where I chose to do it. But it was exceptional good luck that Louise Spindler saw in the finished product the possibility of launching a new series that was to become the *Case Studies in Education and Culture*, parallel to the Spindlers' already successful *Case Studies in Cultural Anthropology*.

Having a mentor who was actively writing and editing books of his own has proved extremely fortuitous throughout my entire career. Spindler continued to create publishing opportunities for me. If I could wish for something good to happen to students everywhere, it would be that they find a mentor who is actively publishing and is willing to see that his or her students find similar opportunities.

The idea of applying for sabbatical leave and making something of it is an opportunity that most academics face at least once, but little is achieved without some purpose in mind, and I must confess that I took my first sabbatical with the best of intentions but no clear way to achieve them in mind. Luck found me in Africa and in a city where I had the good fortune to meet with an anthropologist-administrator who was key to my being allowed (even encouraged!) to study there, and I happened to bite off just what I could chew in the time I had available. By then I was developing a pretty good sense of what I could accomplish, but I have always assumed that things would go well for me, and that part was serendipity. I also was lucky in finding a willing publisher at a university interested in publishing a book about drinking that was definitely not in my field.

The role that administrators play in our lives should be noted, for upon my return to the university after sabbatical, my academic life was up for grabs. My assignment to "shadow" a large demonstration project proved, in the long run, to be fortuitous. And again, the group of resisting teachers in the setting were as cordial as an outsider could hope for and taught me a lesson in the power of teacher resistance.

Fieldwork is essentially an activity of the young, and after aggressively pursuing it for some twenty-five years, I was ready to sit back and reflect. What great good luck to have a publisher invite me to prepare a monograph about writing that set me on a new path. That is "career serendipity," and for me it occurred at an optimum time, when I was ready to explore new arenas.

All these things seemed to come along at just the right moment, and I made of them whatever I could. Maybe I am wrong to think of it as luck, but it seems to me that at best I only had a hand in most of it. Luck, coupled with a lot of patience.

CHAPTER 4
Organizing An Ethnographic Account

With a clear sense of purpose and focus, how do you put everything together to achieve an end result that will accommodate what you have in mind for your ethnography?

Infrastructure today is the way we refer globally to systems that connect things, like highways, bridges, trains, water supply facilities. We don't have a word that refers to the connectors in our written accounts unless we use the term structure itself, referring to the "structure of an argument," "structure of a poem" or the like.

In this chapter I discuss the structure of my ethnographies, drawing on the set of writings you have been following here, in the same order that they occurred in the course of my career. These are not intended as rigid templates. They describe four specific ways that I put my studies together. Since they cover a wide range of topics, they may help you either with the specific approach that I used or help you understand that there is really no end to how you might go about this.

My first example is an unfortunate one: I had absolutely no structure in mind for how the writing was to proceed, even as the fieldwork was drawing to a close. If this situation is comparable to your own, let me suggest that you keep the approach simple and direct as I did.

65

A Kwakiutl Village and Its School:
Cultural Barriers to Classroom Performance

Throughout the period of my fieldwork among the Kwakiutl (September 1962–August 1963) I kept wondering how to go about writing up my dissertation.[1] Spindler wrote encouraging words along those lines, although he was only encouraging me to inform *him* how I intended to approach the writing. I did not have a clue. Suddenly all those ethnographies I had been reading failed to provide the model I needed for how to tell my story. And anyway, in those days we didn't think of ourselves as storytellers. No, this account had to be based on objective observations. I wasn't certain that I had made any.

The only possibility I could see was to ferret out some dominant categories that might provide a way to present the details of what I had seen and experienced. It did seem clear that I should keep my classroom observations separate from the activities of villagers, for they were worlds apart. That is the approach I decided to follow, first relating how the village appeared to be organized to carry out daily routines and seasonal activities. I realized that I could say far more about the pupils and the classroom than I would ever understand about the village, so I better start with the villagers and make that part of the account as strong as possible. How had daily life in the village been carried out prior to my arrival? Clearly that should constitute the essence of my study, and would complement whatever I had to say about the school.

As I sorted my notes about village life, I kept the major headings in Felix Keesing's then recently published book, *Cultural Anthropology: The Science of Custom* (Keesing 1958), in mind. His book was pretty much THE text at Stanford during the years I had just spent there (he was chair of the anthropology department at the time). Some of his headings, such as Economic Organization and Political Organization, gave me pause. I knew that I had little information pertaining to them. I began by stating what I could about the categories that I understood. I hoped that critical readers (i.e., my committee members) would find that sufficient.

By the time I did get to writing about the school and classroom I was pretty much on a roll. I devoted the entire year to writing the dissertation, with nothing to interfere. I had returned to the seaside town of Carmel where I had formerly taught and still had many friends. I was feeling good about the way the study was going, especially the part about the school. My friends were very supportive of my effort, and my dear friend Anna Kohner volunteered to read aloud for me the sections already written—a remarkable help to any writer, especially a beginning one,

I set out to write one chapter a month and got a head start because my first chapter was quite short. (More recently I have advised students not to start writing the first chapter unless they have a crystal clear idea where they are headed. Better to leave it for last, after they have found their sense of direction.) I managed to stay pretty much on schedule.

As I approached the conclusion of my writing task, I decided to highlight the lives of several pupils, presented as little case studies. I had no such plan in mind while I was at the village, so those little studies were not as rich as they might have been. I was not trying to pad the study, however, for I realized that I still had to make some attempt at analysis. I struggled to fulfill the promise of my subtitle by identifying whatever "cultural barriers to classroom performance" I felt I had observed and experienced. The completed dissertation was 511 pages—I was already taking my place as an entrenched over-writer, someone whose writing would always need to be condensed.

In revising the study for publication for the new Spindler series, *Case Studies in Education and Culture,* I essentially kept the structure that I had followed in the dissertation, which at least had achieved its objective as a *completed* dissertation. A few readers even commended it for being well written.

Spindler wanted that the cases in his new series to be short, setting the limit at about 110 printed pages. I came up with 132 pages, which he accepted. And with that much cutting, the manuscript improved considerably. The Kwakiutl book remains in print, having survived four publishers. The most recent reprinting (Wolcott 2003a) contains a postscript added in 1989 plus a poignant statement written by a woman living at the village in 1963.

I am extremely flattered that the book has remained in print so long. The people described in it seem to come alive for new readers, and their problems as Indian people are still with us today. Nonetheless, the Kwakiutl people have seen many improvements in the conditions under which they live. For me as author, the book's success served as a remarkable kick-off for the writing part of my academic career.

The Principal Study

By the time the Kwakiutl book was actually published (1967), I was more than halfway through the fieldwork for my next study, *The Man in the Principal's Office*. But before I wrote up that study, I had to complete writing that I had promised Spindler; you have read in chapter 1 how I went about that, and the lesson I heard and finally understood about ethnography. Spindler's incisive but always constructive comments completely reoriented me about how to focus an ethnography. In so doing, they provided a way to organize my work for this next effort. But I simply could not imagine how to deal with so much data, even though I was convinced that my voluminous notes would provide a solid basis for a write-up.

But, as usual serendipity was there, ready to assist with what loomed as a gigantic task: how to sort material that now filled binder upon binder of raw field notes. My problem was how to sort data into major categories that would help me organize the book.

And who happened to be serving on a panel at "AERA" (the annual meeting of the American Educational Research Association, of which I was a member) and was presenting at its meeting in Chicago that year, but sociologist Howard Becker. "Howie" had for years been a major contributor to qualitative research in education and had been invited to serve on a panel to address issues in method, with an emphasis on managing data. In his remarks he addressed my problem directly, "If you are having trouble sorting data, you are probably trying to do two things at once. Sorting data should be simple; don't confound it with efforts to develop theory." Bingo! He had put his finger on my problem!

Sorting data for the principal study had proved problematic because I was trying to accomplish too much at once. Becker's advice was to sort data on the simplest of criteria. For me, that meant: did a particular bit of data (a datum) relate directly to what the case study principal was doing, *as a principal*, or not? Once I had reduced the problem to that simple question, if an item was related to the principal acting in a particular role, how did it do so? And if it did not, to what other facets of behavior did it pertain (e.g., the principal's personal life, his role as father, his active membership in his church)? The addition of other categories of behavior and observation that did not deal directly with the principal (e.g., the school district, the central office, the neighborhood) provided an entirely workable and simple basis for sorting.

In those pre-word processor days, secretaries reflected the amount of status one had, and I had worked up to meriting one-third of a secretary's time, sharing her with two other educational researchers (W. W. "Sandy" Charters and R. O. Carlson). I worked out a coding scheme in which my one-third secretary used the time allocated to me for typing—on half sheets of standard typing paper—each quote, observation, or vignette that I had marked for special attention.

When that huge task of selecting relevant aspects from my running commentary and having them typed and sorted was completed, I had a study just waiting to be written. My categories virtually dictated the major chapter headings I used: the principal's personal history, his school, his daily routines (subdivided into two parts— formal and informal encounters), followed by chapters discussing the routes by which principals become principals (the socialization of a principal) and in turn how the principal serves as a socializer of others (his staff). Two final, more interpretive chapters were concerned with reflections on the training of principals and the critical difference I recognized between their ideal role as principals themselves seemed to envision it and their real role as it appeared to me.

There were some left over materials and some decisions about where and how to introduce the topic of method. Near the end of the book I included a catchall chapter titled "Behind Many Masks" in which I placed the balance of all the leftover quotes from people in different relationships to the principal. I felt those quotes from members of the various subgroups with whom he worked definitely belonged in book. I put them where they seemed to fit in the text whenever I could, and the rest found their way into a concluding chapter. I have never quite been sure whether I succeeded with that chapter, with its appearance as exactly what it was: a catchall.

As to the issue of method, I felt that Spindler himself was missing the point about the importance of ethnography *as method* in educational research. In spite of his earlier admonition in my article for him that "the methodology and introduction per se should be disposed of in no more than 6 pp." in the chapter I had prepared for him, I felt that I should foreground method, making it the focus of my opening chapter in the forthcoming book. I gave that first chapter what I felt was a fitting title, "A Principal Investigator in Search of a Principal," in a light-hearted reference to the fact that the individual in charge on any project is always referred to as the *principal investigator.*

And there you have it—how the study came to be organized as it was. Spindler liked it and wanted it for his still-new series, *Case Studies in Education and Culture* in spite of its length. The book was published in 1973 and remains in print today in an updated version. It has been translated for distribution in Taiwan and in mainland China (2001, 2009). I had to explain to one patient translator that I doubted that a joke the principal often repeated could be satisfactorily translated into Chinese. In the tale, a principal sends a note home with a student that says, "Johnny smells bad. Can you do something about it?" The note that he receives back says simply, "Don't smell him. Just larn him!"

The study continues to serve inspiration for those interested in examining other educator roles, but inadvertently I had staked out territory as exclusively my own in studying principals. Rather than replicate my efforts by studying other principals—those, for example, who are not Protestant males or who are aggressively upwardly bound—my account gives an incomplete picture of the principalship. We would have been greatly advantaged by having numerous studies providing more instances of that full range that Margaret Mead wrote about.

This reveals the common misunderstanding that one case speaks for all. It is further reinforced by an unfortunate belief perpetuated among graduate students that every dissertation proposal must be unique. My student Jean Campbell did toy with the idea of studying "the woman in the principal's office" but was unable to find a willing principal among the few women who held the position at the time (1986).

The African Beer Gardens of Bulawayo: Integrated Drinking in a Segregated Society

On my sabbatical, I realized the value of having thought about ethnography's basic ingredients. After a few weeks of bumbling about during my search for a suitable subject in what was then Rhodesia, I found myself embarked on the fascinating and formally approved project described in the previous chapter. That was when I happened upon the anthropologist-cum-administrator Hugh Ashton, under whose auspices the African beer gardens of Bulawayo were operated. In exchange for permission to conduct the proposed study, I had promised to submit a copy of my working paper prior to my departure.

I had willingly taken on a project of unknown depth in a climate not lacking in elements of suspicion and distrust between Whites and Blacks, and with an impossible time frame. At best I realized that I would have to scale down my ambitions to see what I could accomplish under the circumstances. No matter what the outcome, I did want the results to have the solid feel of ethnography about them, for it was a decidedly more traditional ethnography that I felt I needed to do next. I could not imagine a better or more exotic site for gaining such experiences than where I happened to be: in Africa.

Yet how to proceed? I could not make one particular beer garden the center of my attention. That would have been impossible under the circumstances. (I did not speak either of the local indigenous languages, and my repeated presence would have raised untoward suspicions among people already superstitious and discontented with many aspects of their lives). I felt I should look at the whole set of practices surrounding the beer gardens, including life in the gardens, the making and selling of beer, how the profits were used, any problems that drinking provoked, the varied opinions about whether it was a legitimate thing for a community to do, and how it all seemed to add up.

But for such an undertaking, I needed some categories into which I could sort data as I uncovered them. Further, if any of my categories seemed to come up short, that might guide me to where I should put my efforts next. I realized that my document would at best be incomplete, but through my outsider perspective I might come up with something of general interest and raise a few questions for insiders to think about.

I turned to four organizing categories I had worked with during the principal study, broad areas that I saw as critical for any well-rounded ethnography:

ENVIRONMENTAL FACTORS: both historical and physical

SOCIAL FACTORS: how people group and align themselves

CULTURAL FACTORS: their belief systems, expectations, world view

INDIVIDUAL BEHAVIORS: how individuals in various roles are affected

Fleshing out these headings gave me a way to get started, and guided the fieldwork. And the categories themselves, in that same order, eventually found their way into my final table of contents.

Environmental factors provided an opportunity to examine historically what had prompted the development of municipal beer gardens; the current size of the local operation; the process of brewing and distributing beer; and the organization of people who had administrative responsibility for managing it, from the head, who watched over the entire organization, and his subordinates, who formed a predominantly White group of administrators and supervisors, to the unit managers, servers, and patrons, all African, at each of the thirty-one beer gardens operated by Bulawayo's Housing and Amenities Department.

Social factors included the groups in which people aligned themselves, for it was not only beer drinkers who used the gardens as a meeting place. The gardens were used by many others for both business and casual purposes. People who frequented the gardens could be categorized in any number of ways: obviously by gender, roughly by age estimates, and not so obviously by whether they were employed or not, their incomes, whether they were rural visitors or urban township dwellers, their highest level of formal education, the hours when they came to the beer garden, whether or how often they drank heavily, who regularly substituted beer drinking for one or more meals, how they felt about the quality and easy availability of the beer, and which gardens they preferred.

Cultural factors took into account the reasons people gave for going to the beer garden and their traditions and beliefs about beer drinking, including its association with life-cycle and ceremonial events, and changing patterns of beer use, especially among young men.

I was interested in collecting personal stories, including stories of drinkers and non-drinkers, young and old, men (and women—the hardest group for me to reach). I counted heavily on shoring up gaps in my study by gathering as many different accounts as I could, for I was beginning to appreciate the importance of individual experiences with drinking and with the beer gardens. Of course what was there called "European" beer, like the beer Americans are accustomed to, was popular but beyond the financial means of most. Drinking was left largely to adult men, but because minors under the age of nineteen were technically prohibited in the beer gardens, it was a coup for them to be seen there.

Attending to *individual behaviors*, including everyone whose life was in one way or another affected by the presence of the beer gardens, proved a good way to build my account, and it meant that I did not have to spend a lot of time in the beer gardens. (My presence was always accompanied by a White supervisor, was always conspicuous, and I was obliged to observe the custom of White staff, tasting enough beer to attest to its quality and thus allaying an ever-present concern that it contained suspicious additives.) I listened to anyone with an opinion about why the beer was so easily available.

Potential informants for my study included medical doctors and hospital staff, churchmen, non-drinkers among Whites as well as Blacks, African welfare workers (whose salaries were paid out of beer profits), the police, and immediate supervisors. I recorded a wide range of opinion in every group; I explored the range without making any claim as to the randomness of my responses.

Along the way, I refueled my interest in culture acquisition when I got to the topic of becoming a drinker. That was one part of my study in which my longstanding interest dovetailed with my new project. Among my final chapters is one titled "Becoming A Drinker."

I did not have a finished manuscript in hand when I returned from my sabbatical in 1971, although I had a good start on one. Eventually I completed the rewrite. I was encouraged when editor Mark Keller at the Rutgers Center of Alcohol Studies expressed interest, but he seemed to be telling me he was sorry he did not have sufficient funds available to be able to publish. How was I to know that he meant only that he did not have funds *at that very moment?* Once he secured funds, he notified me that he was ready and excited about publishing the book, in spite of the projected cost of including several photos of my own and several of the public-relations type gladly furnished by the Department of Housing and Amenities.

The book's subtitle, "Integrated Drinking in a Segregated Society," was intended to point to the fact that drinking was well integrated in African society; it was Rhodesian society itself that remained segregated.

Teachers Versus Technocrats: An Educational Innovation in Anthropological Perspective

Meanwhile, at the federally funded research center where I was employed, there had been some major redirection from Washington, D.C. The Center's mission was now to initiate projects directly intended to assist schools with efforts at improvement, and all the Center's funds had been fully allocated. There was no research role for an anthropologist in the Center's activities, and if I was to stay on board, I would have to be assigned to some already existing project.

The Center's director, Max Abbott, now had a better idea of what I might do that resembled what he understood, on the basis of my principal study, that ethnographers do. As recounted in the previous chapter, the biggest project the center was underwriting was patterned after the program, planning and budgeting systems then popular with the federal government, to see how tighter planning and greater accountability might improve teaching practice. A set of materials developed along these lines was currently undergoing a test of effectiveness in a demonstration project being conducted in a nearby school district.

The program had a formal evaluation team standing by with plans to measure its effectiveness, but the director saw in me a way that he might learn how the program was going other than having to wait for the final report or hear only through glowing accounts from the developers themselves. I realized that the whole assignment might result in a paper prepared for a single reader, but I also realized it would be a grave error to insist that I was overqualified for the task.

I had an agenda of my own. My concern was to make my next assignment, whatever it turned out to be, as anthropological as possible, to draw upon anthropology in whatever way I could to show how anthropology had a role to play in educational research.

I found myself heading down the highway in the company of the program developer for my first visit with school personnel: genteel and well meaning folk trying to introduce change in a school district comprised of one high school, one middle school, and several feeder schools in a semi-rural community. The meeting was upbeat and cordial, with highly favorable reports from the only attending principal, one teacher from his school, and other central office personnel. There was but brief mention of an informal teacher committee somewhere in the district that seemed to be offering a bit of resistance. I took my cue from that offhand comment and decided to begin my inquiry with that group—provided that I could find them. And there begins my tale.

I discovered that I had walked into a hornet's nest of angry teachers frustrated by the time the new project consumed, the demands it placed upon them, the manner in which it had been implemented, and even questions as to what the University and the Center were up to, since some of the district's own administrators seemed hell-bent on defending the program, oblivious to teacher complaints. What was the point of it all?

My heart skipped a beat. Here was a story just waiting to be told—a rift in the school district which my colleagues in the research center were causing but of which they remained for the most part totally unaware. I would have a story simply by recording what was happening. But remember, I had been a classroom teacher for five years, including now the additional one among the Kwakiutl. My teacher instincts were alerted; I smelled a rat. I realized that I could not look impartially into a situation that was causing teachers so much anguish, even if my own R&D colleagues were partly to blame for the problem. Although I recognized my leaning toward the teachers' side, I also recognized the intent of upwardly mobile administrators to forge a closer working relationship with the university and to create the image of a small rural district (read "superintendent") ready and willing to have teachers explore something new.

I approached the teacher group and inquired whether they would allow me to sit in on their deliberations. I had to warn them that I would be no help to their cause, since my work would not be completed until the project was "finished"—one way or the other—but they seemed to take heart from my presence and hoped that some good might come simply from having their side of the story documented. They welcomed whatever attention I could bring.

When the time came, it provided my opportunity to draw on anthropology in a different way—to try to locate something in the literature that would help me maintain sufficient objectivity to carry out the research. Together with the assistance of a member of the anthropology department at the university (Professor Phil Young), we examined the anthropological concept of *moiety* in the literature on social organization and whether it seemed apropos for looking at the situation at hand

The word moiety comes from the French and means "half," referring to one of something that has only two parts. Thus a society with a moiety form of social organization has two (and only two) groups, each of which performs some tasks for the other that it does not perform for itself, in addition to performing tasks necessary for the group as a whole. After combing the literature, I could explain that in a moiety form of social organization both halves of the division are necessary. Each group carries out some functions unique to itself, carries out some functions for the good of the entire society, and carries out some functions for the other half of the group that it does not perform for itself.

Those conditions seemed to prevail in the circumstance I was witnessing. I planned to show how the two groups that I was observing—one composed primarily of teachers, the other consisting of administrators, researchers, and other like-minded souls—showed a similar arrangement, and let the literature guide me to find parallel functions akin to those described in the classic literature. As I saw it, those two groups bore a remarkable resemblance to moieties in the performance of their duties.

I proceeded with my research, informed by the idea of moieties, prompting a parallel in this case with the two groups as I came to call them: the "teachers," and those I labeled the "technocrats." The latter consisted of most (not all!) administrators and central office staff, plus anyone aspiring to (and empathizing with) the concerns of administrators. It also included my colleagues in the research center—all devoted educators but concerned that the schools were not doing an adequate job and that the problem was primarily with teachers. They were the kind of educators anxious to develop "teacher-proof" materials, those responsible today for programs like No Child Left Behind.

The project lasted three additional years beyond its official termination, and as one member of the teacher committee noted, "It took them about three years to get it in; looks like it will take us about three years to get rid of it." In the tradition of long term fieldwork, I was able to "stick around" for years four, five, and six of a project originally designed only for years one, two, and three.

My final Table of Contents begins with an overview of the operation of the pilot program, how the teachers were directed to prepare their lessons and how they were to record student progress. Next I wrote a brief discussion of moieties and how they operated, straight out of the anthropology literature. Then I examined how the behavior of actors in either of the two groups could be viewed *as if* they were moieties.

And that is how I organized the account related in *Teachers versus Technocrats: An Educational Innovation in Anthropological Perspective* (1977). That account has also been republished in an updated version (2003d).

Sneaky Kid and Its Aftermath

The institutional impetus for the Sneaky Kid project, the next of my studies, came from an invitation from the U.S. Office of Education (at the time the National Institute of Education, NIE) to write a paper on the topic of *educational adequacy.* The core idea was to have contributors suggest alternative ways to distribute "equalization" monies among schools that would result in a balanced allocation of funds to schools in need. Needless to say, I suspected (correctly) that such funds would never became available, and anyway it looked to me like a problem for economists. I declined the invitation.

But whoever was calling me from Washington, D.C., insisted that there were already enough economists writing on the subject. What they wanted was the view of sociologists like me. "But I'm more of an anthropologist," I insisted. "That's okay, too," came the reply, and I was hooked.

I realized that I could indeed write about the broader topic of educational adequacy, for at the time I had a

school-leaver living on my property, a young man who had
already found our educational system lacking. "If I can
get him to tell me his story," I thought, "then I might have
something to contribute—about a problem even more fun-
damental than the allocation of equalization funds!" And
that is how it all got started.

I liked the idea of doing a life story, although I had
never written one. The possibility of this one rested totally
on Brad's (a pseudonym) willingness to cooperate; to my
surprise, he was willing to give it a try. He estimated that
it would take him about twelve hours to fully recount his
story, and I thought his estimate reasonable. But when I
set up the tape recorder and asked him to begin his nar-
rative, it took him only twelve minutes from start to finish
to complete his account, and I realized that doing a life
history was not such a snap after all. From that point we
worked for up to an hour at a time over several weeks. (I
do not recall exactly how long we worked at this, but he
was paid for his time and seemed fairly satisfied when he
read the results).

From the outset I assumed that I would follow the
chronology of Brad's life as he related it, but there did not
seem to be any order to his account. As he recalled inci-
dents from his life he explained them in detail, but nothing seemed to link up. I realized that to make sense of
his story I would need some internal organizers, either
major events in his life or major categories of behavior. I
began to reorder and to move things about, so that I could
make sense in retelling his story. In doing this, I mentioned that I worked with a "heavy hand." And I truly felt
that I had, but I did not introduce any changes in his style
of speaking or in reporting exactly what he said. I did not
understand at the time why a few readers were perplexed

at this way of handling the data. Have they ever taken a close look at the way most people relate personal stories?

Because this project was ostensibly school related, I kept all Brad's school-relevant remarks together, although needless to say, there weren't a lot of them. Most of Brad's account was about growing up and being shuffled about among relatives and about the more daring things he had done as a youth. And it was a story singularly about Brad, with no other person—family or friend—close enough personally to interact with him.

Although I felt that I had edited with a heavy hand with the liberties I took to rearrange Brad's words, I did not intend to write with one. I began to wonder how one's use of titles and subtitles plays a role in directing a reader's attention. Ultimately, in organizing the account, I used as few major subheadings as possible, focusing attention on the main part of the story, subtitled "In the Chute." I found this phrase in a talk given at a meeting of the American Correctional Association, in which a speaker had remarked, "People who are in the chute, so to speak, and heading toward us, are beginning that movement down in infancy." That assessment resonated with me—I wondered if that aptly described Sneaky Kid; to this day, I still wonder if Brad was already "in the chute" (see Wolcott 2010).

In the article I introduce Brad and explain how we happened to find each other, and then I turn to the major section. In that part of the account I introduce topics with brief, unassuming margin headings suggested by the material that followed, using Brad's own words wherever possible.

This section, titled "In the Chute," contains material with the following subheads:

On the loose
Getting busted
Second rate jobs and second rate apartments
A new life
Picking up what was needed
The bicycle thief
Being sneaky
I don't have to steal, but ...
Breaking and entering
Inching closer to the chute
I'm not going to get caught
Home is the hunter
Growing up
Getting paid for dropping out
Hiding out from life

The next heading dealt with what I called "Worldview: Getting My Life Together" and includes the following:

A job—That's all that makes you middle class
Building my own life
Being by myself
Friends
I've been more places and done more things
Some personal standards
Moderation: Getting close enough,
    going 'medium' fast
Putting it all together

A final section was devoted to Brad's thoughts about, and experiences with, formal schooling. That was followed by interpretive comments in a section that reiterated the major title, "Adequate Schools and Inadequate Education: An Interpretation." These headings, downplayed as they were, allowed me to present Brad without painting him as good or evil. I doubt that the same labels in the same order would fit in other cases, but you might consider them a template for how you could organize your own case, allowing your informant to supply the labels for subtitles.

Summary of this Lesson: How to Tell Your Story

The purpose of this chapter has not been to provide four *specific* ways to organize an account but to underscore that there are innumerable ways to go about it, not the least of which is to tell it like it actually happened. I have intended to show that there are many logics you might draw upon: logics of the case itself, logics in the categories you choose, logics in variations in the way often suggested for presenting any account ("first you tell them what you are going to tell them, then you tell them, and then you tell them what you told them").

You might think of these alternatives as features variously derived from the sources available to you:

Chronologically framed units (seasonal, weekly, hourly) derived from on-going activities

Categories derived from the setting(s)

Categories derived from the literature

A set of sequential categories of your own design that lead logically to your conclusion

If the account seems to lack a natural starting place, you must create one. If the activity is ongoing, stop it anywhere that suits you and that gives enough of a toe hold to get going, And if you really feel stumped, share your problem with your readers and put yourself at their mercy: "I could never figure out exactly where to begin this account, so somewhat arbitrarily I will begin at the point where…"

CHAPTER FIVE
Searching for Ethnography's Essence

I have spent a good part of my life looking for the "essence" of ethnography, so that my students and I would have a standard against which we could assess efforts of our own, as well as judge the efforts of others in determining the critical categories that we expected to see covered in any report that claims to be ethnographic. That search informed my lecturing and writing about ethnography and has occupied much of my professional thought. I never found a ready made list that precisely spelled out the requirements, because, of course, there is no magic list, but I think I have come close enough to a workable list to get my work done.

This lesson recounts the story about that search. It is not a dramatic search of the Indiana Jones type, but an academic search about as exciting as looking something up in the library. As you may recall from chapter 4, the idea of having at least some major categories in mind was most helpful when I was thinking about how to study beer gardens in Bulawayo.

The idea for conducting the search and writing about ethnography first came about at a lunch meeting in November 1995, more than fifteen years ago. I had just published a book with Mitch Allen, at the time editor and publisher of

AltaMira Press. Mitch had suggested the meeting for what I thought was to be a celebration of achievement, but instead he began our conversation with his usual question, "What are you going to write for us next?"

Directly or indirectly, Mitch Allen has been responsible for many of the books that I have published. His question has always been the same. He always waited about five seconds for my answer, and, if I didn't have something in mind, he would present the idea *he* had in mind. Since my work previous to that point had dealt with aspects of qualitative research, he jumped in with the suggestion that this time I might write specifically about *ethnography*.

I liked the idea and the challenge. I have been learning about and doing ethnography for more than fifty years, and I have been writing and teaching about it for almost that long. Writing a book would give me a chance to share what I had learned, and help to further a cause I share with a number of others: to keep ethnography intact as a clearly identifiable style of research, rather than watch it become just another synonym for qualitative research in general. Toward that end I had been goaded by comments made by colleagues so anxious to make ethnography user friendly that they simply tossed it in with all the other forms of qualitative research. It was becoming indistinguishable. They seemed to me to fail to appreciate, and thus try to preserve, what is unique about ethnography, what particular contribution it has to make.

I think the first person that I was aware of who treated it as "just another synonym for qualitative research" was my colleague Louis M. Smith, professor of educational psychology at Washington University, St. Louis. His remarks alone would have served as my inspiration, had not the same idea reappeared often in the words of other qualitative researchers in related fields. In 1978, Louis Smith wrote about "the genre of research that is coming to be known by such varied labels as educational ethnography, participant observation, qualitative observation, case study, or field study" and then concluded his observation with the statement, "For the most part, I will use these terms as synonyms" (Smith 1978:316).

Lou Smith made a substantial contribution to qualitative research, and he wanted other researchers to feel comfortable with it as well, and to recognize the many similarities among qualitative approaches. I had endeavored to keep colleagues from becoming *too* comfortable.[1] Though not totally incompatible, my intent has been to preserve whatever unique contribution ethnography has to make, conceptual as well as methodological.

This is still a concern for me, for in the earliest draft of my new book, *Ethnography: A Way of Seeing*, editor Mitch Allen took me to task for writing that seemed to render ethnography inaccessible for all but a select few, a group he estimated at "about thirty people, worldwide." Mitch wanted me to help (my, as well as his) readers who were interested in learning more about ethnography, not to tell them that they weren't really doing it. In revising the draft, I hope I succeeded in that task without losing sight of my original objective, to show that there is something special and particular about ethnography. I meant to present ethnography as special but not inaccessible.

What Makes A Study "Ethnographic"?

But what is it that makes ethnography special? What is it that one can rightfully expect when the claim is to ethnography rather than to some other methodological scheme, such as conversation analysis, symbolic interactionism, or ethnomethodology, or to a generic name that does not implicate a particular disciplinary link, such as participant observer study, case study, or naturalistic inquiry?

What makes a study ethnographic? And, when does it matter whether or not it is truly ethnographic? If you wanted to make a study more ethnographic, what would you have to do? I have never felt that I had really pinned down the essence of ethnography so that I could explain what any particular study had, or needed more of, to qualify for the label. Writing the proposed book allowed, encouraged, in a way forced me to tease out an ethnographic essence. I accepted Mitch's challenge as a way to think about and define genuine ethnography.

That is more or less what I was up to during those years immediately prior to 1999, fleshing out a proposed outline for the book, then building an inventory of critical attributes as I went along. I began by reviewing a tentative list of attributes as I started isolating them and adding to my expanding inventory. In all, I identified a dozen attributes one can reasonably expect to find in ethnographic reporting. The list could be shorter or longer; for my purposes, twelve seemed enough (and anyway, as noted, I have a propensity to think in threes or multiples of three). I will say a bit about these attributes and how each of them fits into the overall picture.

This was never intended as a technical list; you will hardly hear an unfamiliar term or unexpected idea. In one sense we all do all the time what ethnographers do some of the time, except that we do it to accomplish our individual purposes rather than to render descriptions of the collective social behavior of others. And let me suggest a very straightforward purpose for ethnography: we conduct our studies in order to examine how others manage the organization of their lives. It is our way of examining human potential.

For the moment I will not address problems that some of these attributes raise for the fieldworker. Subsequently, I will revisit the list for that purpose. Nor is there any particular order in the way I present or discuss these attributes. It is simply a collection of reasonable expectations about what one can expect to find in any ethnography.

I began by recalling an anthropologist who summarized in a talk that anthropology is *holistic*, *cross-cultural*, and *comparative*. Since ethnography is the field arm of cultural anthropology, ethnography ought to exhibit those same qualities, so I began my inventory with those three attributes.

1. Ethnography is *holistic*. Perhaps the term holistic is no longer in vogue. Better is the idea that ethnography is especially sensitive to context, and to multiple contexts. I am greatly influenced by the idea of human behavior as "overdetermined," that we should always consider multiple causes and influences on our actions (see Wolcott 2010).

2. Ethnography is *cross-cultural*. Ethnography is the study of The Other, some other group's way of life. Hard to argue with that as a general descriptor, although these days what satisfies the criterion as to what is cross-cultural enough is more tenuous than in the good old days.

3. Ethnography is *comparative*. Everything we do and understand is based on comparison. Being cross-cultural is one way of providing comparison. But ethnography is comparative in multiple ways, not endlessly listing similarities and differences, but, as anthropologist Clifford Geertz stated long

ago, looking for "systematic relationships among diverse phenomena, not for substantive identities among similar ones" (Geertz 1973:44).

With those three points to establish a base, it was relatively easy to identify a number of other attributes as my search progressed. Eventually, I identified nine additional attributes that, when taken together, seem to capture the essence I was looking for. Indeed, initially it seemed hard to imagine ethnography without each and every one of them.

4. Ethnographers work from *authentic,* first-hand experience. The ethnographer has been there, the reporting is personal. Fieldwork is sometimes described as "living one's way into a culture." The ethnographer takes himself or herself to be the primary instrument for data collection. And what could possibly be a better instrument for observing human behavior? True, we are chided by colleagues from other disciplines who wonder that we go about making up our own data. But isn't that preferable to depending entirely on data made up by someone else?

5. Ethnography is *real,* it is conducted in natural settings. There is nothing contrived in the behavior ethnographers observe and record, there are no control groups, no hypothetical situations; just people acting as they act in everyday settings. How people really act, as well as how they say they act, or how they say they ought to act, are what interests us.

6. Ethnography assumes an *intimate,* long-term acquaintance. Time works its advantage for the

ethnographer. No one can keep up an "appearance" forever, so the ethnographer eventually sees things as they really are. James Clifford describes ethnography as "an especially deep, extended, and interactive research encounter" (1997:187). It has also been described less pretentiously as "deep hanging out" (Renato Rosaldo, quoted in Clifford 1997:188).

7. Ethnography is *non-judgmental*. Deferred judgment is the order of the day. The ethnographer wants to see how things are, not to judge how they ought to be. To understand how things fit together to form patterns. The ethnographer is not there to judge.

8. Ethnography is basically *descriptive;* and thick description is obviously better than thin. Consistent with deferred judgment, the reporting is based on what is observed, not how people in the setting or how the ethnographer might wish it could be. What you see is what you report, without embellishment: the "eyes" have it.

9. Ethnography is *specific*. It is local and particular—particular people in particular places at a particular time. It is grounded in instances of specific observed behavior. It is about somebody, not about everybody. [After reading chapter 1 you may have an idea where this notion came from!]

10. Ethnography is flexible, *adaptive*. The ethnographer works with an "open" research design (if, indeed, there is any design at all, other than a statement of purpose continually being refined as the work proceeds). The assumption is that until

you are present in the setting, you may not discover what an appropriate question is or how to approach it. For the ethnographer, data shape the theory, not the other way around.

One sometimes hears the process described as "dialectic," as in Michael Agar's statement that ethnography is "dialectic, not linear" (1980:9). I am taken with his description of ethnography as a *selective narrowing* of focus, what Agar refers to as the "funnel approach" when he writes:

> In ethnography...you learn something ("collect some data"), then you try to make sense out of it ("analysis"), then you go back and see if the interpretation makes sense in light of new experience ("collect more data"), then you refine your interpretation ("more analysis"), and so on. The process is dialectic, not linear. [Agar 1980:9; repeated in Agar 1996:62]

11. Ethnography is *corroborative*. A canon of good fieldwork is that you don't rely on single sources of data. A popular term for this is "triangulation." It is so popular that I have heard overly enthusiastic graduate students describe triangulation as the method they intend to follow. How checking up on your data or confirming your sources could ever become a method is beyond me, but that doesn't mean you don't check your sources. [In a fieldwork seminar, one might go so far as to declare that we would never report data that have not been confirmed. I seriously doubt that any experienced fieldworker would attest to that statement, however.]

12. Ethnography is *idiosyncratic* and individualistic. The approach fits with an ethos of self-reliance and independence—traditional ethnography has most often been accomplished by one person who takes full responsibility for a study, from proposal to final write-up. No two studies are ever exactly alike, and each study bears the stamp of the person who conducts it. Since there are cultural scenes aplenty, there is no need for anyone to go to the exact same place to study the exact same thing at the exact same time. Traditionally, even restudies have usually been conducted by the person who did the original fieldwork.

Making the List Better

As my writing continued and I continued to tease out different attributes, I assumed my list would become more concise. Relatively minor points would be subsumed to make major ones stronger. Eventually the list would be boiled down to a few powerful characteristics I could declare as containing the essence of ethnography.

But that is not what happened. As my list grew longer at one end, a shadow of doubt began to form over the qualities already identified. Each characteristic that seemed essential to ethnography had some special conditions or problems attached to it, a downside or caution that weakened the case that it was absolutely essential as an attribute. Let me go back over my list again, this time in a more critical light that questions whether each of the criteria identified is characteristic of *every* ethnography, an absolute necessity without which the ethnographic claim cannot be made.

1. Ethnography is holistic. This seems a worthy goal to strive for, sage counsel to offer a fieldworker. But it is not much of a criterion for evaluating a study. You can be caught out either way. If you are too focused, you are subject to the criticism that you have not provided sufficient context; if you attend too closely to context, you are subject to the criticism that you did not focus adequately. Basically the concern is one of balance in terms of the purposes of the study, the storyteller's dilemma of just how wide a swath to cut. When endeavoring to attend to balance, perhaps the best strategy is to do what you as an individual observer do best, variously emphasizing focus *or* context as your purposes allow, but capitalizing on your own forte. For the ethnographer, the haunting words that anthropology could become nothing more than history might make us want to insure that our accounts are always something more than history.

2. Ethnography is cross-cultural. We recognize that ethnography got its start in cross-cultural study, and we recognize how ideal it would be if everyone interested in pursuing ethnography either could experience another cultural setting or could initially pursue fieldwork in such a setting. But several things mitigate this:

- it is not practical for everyone wanting to do ethnography to have prior experience in a dramatically different culture.

- opportunities for cross cultural experience are limited even for those with time and inclination, and there is resistance in some groups to having ethnographers among them.

- outside the discipline of anthropology, the groups we might want to study are often groups in which we ourselves hold membership: educational researchers studying schools, nurses studying hospitals or health givers, an in-house ethnographer studying social relations within the firm, etc.

❧ with terms like "autoethnography" floating about, it might even be assumed (incorrectly) that these days one can do ethnography on (or "of") oneself.

Cross-cultural settings may have been where the action was, but today we've brought our methods home. Even for the anthropologist, the ideal of prior cross-cultural study in a dramatically different society remains something of a desirable but not always obtainable goal. In the absence of dramatic cultural differences, today we make more of micro-cultural differences, recognizing, with anthropologist Ward Goodenough, that we all participate in multiple cultural systems, and therefore multiculturalism is the "normal human experience" (1976).

Alas, recognizing that the workers in your local supermarket, restaurant, or firehouse all have "cultures" of their own somehow lacks the dramatic aspects of the kind of perspective that a Margaret Mead or Branislaw Malinowski—or Indiana Jones—could bring to their work. We console ourselves that where ethnographers once sought to make the strange familiar, today's ethnographer more often needs to make the familiar strange.

3. Ethnography is comparative. But if ethnography is supposed to be comparative, what is it that one is supposed to compare? Cross-cultural comparison was at one time the marching order of the day. Matter of fact, in an era of armchair anthropology, when the dialogue depended on the first hand reports of others—such as missionaries or adventurers—endless comparisons were made of peoples among whom the scholars themselves had no firsthand experience.

That kind of comparison went out of fashion years ago, and precisely how we employ comparison today baffles me. I have been inclined to advise beginning fieldworkers to do as little comparing as possible rather than as much. Comparison tends to draw one's attention away from what is being observed. In itself, comparison can become an endless, as well as pointless, preoccupation.

In American anthropology a distinction is made between ethnography and ethnology. Ethnography is the description of the way of life of one human group, ethnology the comparison of two or more such groups. Since virtually everything we do is comparative anyway, I feel that explicit comparison is best left for another time or other circumstances. Your task as ethnographer is to attend to careful description—at least until you go on to conduct a second or third inquiry of your own; or, to study one group over an extended period, as British ethnographers have tended to do.

Comparison is given far too much credence in qualitative research, especially to doing comparisons on a scale that the beginning student can accomplish in conducting a descriptively-oriented master's thesis or doctoral dissertation. Too often I have watched as graduate students are wheedled into "increasing their N's"—that is, to doing two, three, or five little cases instead of restricting their observations to one case studied in depth.

The argument for comparison is the belief that it can make a study stronger or more "scientific." What tends to happen instead is that those larger Ns serve as denominators: they reduce the time that can be devoted to each individual case. If you do three "little" cases, each one will get one-third as much attention as the one might have had if you had focused exclusively on it. That's okay if you want to look for a range of possible practices—but there goes context, for you are likely to find that you are doing little more than conducting a small survey (and let me assure you that ethnography is a very inefficient way to conduct a survey!).

When it does come time to compare, as it inevitably will even as you try to resist, let me remind you again of the words of Clifford Geertz, who recommended that we should "look for systematic relationships among diverse phenomena, not for substantive identities among similar ones'" (1973b:44).

[So here I am, anxious to explicate a tradition that exhorts one to be holistic, cross-cultural, and comparative, yet coming up instead with questions as to whether these attributes are part of the solid foundation upon which contemporary ethnography rests. They are among a number of desirable features often found in ethnography but not critical attributes. Their importance seems to diminish as ethnographic research is adapted to local circumstances. Let me continue to examine some of my list's other shortcomings.]

4. Ethnography is authentic; it reports from first-hand experience. Well, at last we find a feature that is characteristic of *all* ethnography: the presence of the ethnographer in the scene being reported. That's virtually a must!

Except, of course, in those situations where being there is impossible, impractical, illegal, and, alas, sometimes just inconvenient. Ethnographers have often gone to remarkable lengths to "be there," but we can easily think of situations where we do not insist on firsthand observation as the only means for getting information. Studies of prison life or prostitution come quickly to mind, but even for the ethnohistorian there is no way to reach back into the past other than through the "memory cultures" of elderly informants. We may regard this exception as a recent turn of events, ethnographers driving to their field sites early in the morning or even taking the subway. Yet Franz Boas is reported to have waited impatiently in his hotel room at Port Hardy, British Columbia, for his Kwakiutl informants to show up and to fume when they failed to keep their appointments. That was almost a hundred fifty years ago!

And even if you are there—on site and in person—your presence hardly guarantees the accuracy or thoroughness of your data. You can't be everywhere at once, your own biases undoubtedly limit and distort what you do observe, and your very presence makes demands on your time and energy when it entails making arrangements for eating, sleeping, attending to personal matters, and even getting away from the people you are there to study in order to maintain some perspective of your own. If you commute to your site, you lose something of that holistic picture you want to get, but if you reside at the site, invariably you will be beset by factions and petty jealousies simply because wherever you are, you can't be somewhere else.

The idea of "being there" represents an idealistic view of how fieldwork should be conducted, something we can all agree is highly desirable, but often in the cases we know firsthand, impractical. Time alone may preclude the possibility of being there, and maybe there is no "there" there at all, as, for example, studying internet communities that exist without face-to-face interaction, or ham radio operators, or people engaging in telephone sex.

5. Ethnography is real, it is conducted in natural settings. It is certainly correct to say that ethnographers do not attempt to manipulate the settings or situations in which they study, but it is not so easy to establish exactly what constitutes a "natural" setting. Schools, hospitals, prisons, offices, factories, are all such commonplace settings as to seem natural to us, yet there are certainly unnatural qualities about them. Perhaps natural settings are themselves part of our collective memory culture, how things were in the old days, idealized to contrast with the realities of the present. It is our obligation to state the conditions we find; the reader can judge the naturalness of the setting.

We would have to say that there is a strong preference for studying things in their natural state, but we are willing to settle for settings that the ethnographer cannot manipulate and does not control. We may wish we could control them, to keep out other external influences (with the exception of ourselves) and maintain everything in pristine condition. Our efforts in this regard are sometimes transparent, as when we write about a people as though they have little or no contact with the outside world, or write about them in a third-person way that suggests that not even we ourselves were present during the study (a neat trick if you can pull it off).

6. Ethnography requires intimate, long-term acquaintance. Exactly what constitutes an intimate relationship in fieldwork, or how long an acquaintanceship must be to qualify as "long-term" is largely ignored in discussions of fieldwork criteria. So this attribute is rather ill defined, although as a criterion it has a satisfying ring. Perhaps in comparison with other styles of research, we can reach agreement that ethnographers are simply more intimate, their acquaintance more long-term, than that of any other kind of social research. As a broad descriptor, stated comparatively, this one does seem to point in the right direction.

But the terms are not readily operationalized. How intimate is intimate? And is intimacy necessarily desirable when the threat of betrayal lurks in every ethnographic report, revealing things told in confidence or revealing something that embarrasses the informant. Not all ethnographers handle intimacy well or have any wish to become intimate with informants, fearful of the loss of objectivity that they feel professionally obliged to maintain.

Length of time in the field can become a two edged sword; length of stay is no guarantee of better fieldwork. Most of us can act our best selves, at least for awhile. But the longer we stay, the less likely we may be able to keep up a front or play a role. Fieldworkers are therefore as apt to overstay their welcome as to leave too soon. In a sense, the longer you stay, the greater your chances of screwing up the relationship, antagonizing someone, or taking a giant misstep. Mistrust is far easier to achieve than trust.

One possible way to accomplish long-term acquaintance is through an extended period that is not continuous but is achieved through intermittent visits. While that is possible in the course of a career and may be the norm in urban ethnography, it is not the kind of advice one wants to hear when setting out the first time, when attention is more likely to be focused on the *minimum* time necessary. When that question becomes a burning issue, we worry about efforts to short-circuit ethnographic tradition. How do you answer the question, "How short can a long-term study be?"

My most recent study, to be developed in more detail in chapter 6, addresses the intimacy problem—in case study fashion, as you might expect in a book titled *Sneaky Kid and Its Aftermath: Ethics and Intimacy in Fieldwork* (Wolcott 2002). But a caution: I only examine the problem of how intimacy can compromise fieldwork, I do not attempt to resolve it. I have a bit more to say on this sensitive issue in the next chapter where the lesson focuses on issues of intimacy.

7. Ethnography is non-judgmental. The ethnographer is enjoined not to rush to judgment. But it is difficult to withhold judgment, even under the guise of simply inquiring into how other people live. We study The Other, no disrespect intended, but we agonize over what still seems to come down to the privileged position of the observer. We have altered our approach; today we study *with* you; we are careful not to call you our *subjects.* Nor do we like calling you our *informants,* although we nonetheless expect you to inform us. Even our relativistic stance has become relative. As occasion has arisen for ethnographers to accept assignments specifically to assess or to evaluate new programs or changed circumstances, suddenly we admit to being adept at evaluating after all. We attempt to approach such assignments in a different way, however, by keeping our focus on trying to understand what *is* rather than what should be. And we approach our studies without malice.

But we certainly do not want to be left out if evaluation is where the action is. And regardless of an expected professional stance, it is human nature to have preferences, even when it is not politically correct, or even a good idea, to reveal them. Ethnographers have found a way out of the dilemma by contrasting being objective and being neutral, taking the position that one does not need to be neutral in order to be objective. In short, we are capable of making judgments if that is what is wanted, we don't make them if that is what is wanted. "Deferred judgment" proves a handy label, conveniently imprecise, maybe as near as one can come in fieldwork to having one's cake and eating it, too.

8. *Ethnography is descriptive.* The best way to be non-evaluative is to be intensely descriptive, to attend to what is, and what those in the setting think about it, rather than become preoccupied with what is wrong, or with what ought to be. But description is endless; both Margaret Mead and Branislaw Malinowski, two of our most prominent elders, have been accused of "haphazard" descriptiveness (Clifford 1988:32), and anyone who has tried to provide a complete description of anything recognizes that potentially it is a run-away activity (Becker 2007:98-99).

Thick description is clearly better than thin, but what constitutes enough thin description to make it thick? And if we recognize attending to context as one of our special strengths, how far out should we go, to what level of detail, when any attention we give to context detracts from the focus. [Just think how broad the context of the principal's personal world was, and how it differed from his professional world, as described in chapter 1.]

Furthermore, a call for description implies that it is somehow a pure act, that when we describe, we free ourselves from judgments or preconceived ideas. Yet as William James has observed, one can't even pick up rocks in a field without a theory (in Agar 1980:23). Description requires making choices—what is to be described, at what level of detail, while something else is ignored or described with less detail. Pure description has been referred to lightheartedly as the "doctrine of immaculate perception" (Beer 1973). Ethnography puts an emphasis on description, but when you find yourself actually doing it, you may be surprised at how uncertain you are about how to go about it, and how impossible it would be to provide either a pure or a complete description of anything (Becker 2007:98).

Nonetheless, you are likely to end up with more descriptive data than you could ever include. And the more thorough you are, the more likely you are to uncover matters deemed personal and private. So the more you know, the greater the problems you may have in deciding what needs to be reported, what might be reported or omitted, and what definitely should not be reported. So-called basic description is not such an easy path to follow after all.

9. Ethnography is specific. Clifford Geertz described ethnographic description as "microscopic" (Geertz 1973b: 21), stating flatly: "There is no ascent to truth without a corresponding descent to cases." Here is another strength that also may appear initially as a weakness. Our instances are often single instances. "What can you learn from a single case?" we are asked repeatedly.

It took me years to realize that a straightforward answer, somewhat akin to Mead's idea that each of us is a perfect example, an "organic representation" of his or her complete cultural experience (see again chapter 2), should be, "All we can." Our generalizations are always suspect, our efforts at theory huge leaps from what we observe in everyday interaction to universals describing human behavior. In their efforts to stay relevant with the times, one hears today of anthropologists whose specialty is the "ethnography of the state," which I find a curious effort to have it both ways. I feel more comforted by Geertz's consoling words on that score: "It is not necessary to know everything in order to understand something" (1973b: 20).

I think the resolution for ethnographers, and for social scientists of any ilk, was summed up more than sixty years ago by Clyde Kluckhohn and Henry Murray in their edited collection, *Personality in Nature, Society, and Culture* (Kluckhohn and Murray 1948:35), when they wrote [in the gendered language of the day]:

> Every man is in certain respects
> a. like all other men,
> b. like some other men,
> c. like no other man.

What they were saying about individuals holds true for micro-cultures and national cultures as well. Being particularistic feels natural to most ethnographers—but not all ethnographers are alike, so of course neither are their ethnographies. Some approach the groups they study as though there are no individuals in them, only "a people" seeming to act in unison, while others build their accounts around a single individual through the anthropological life history or "ethnographic autobiography" (see Wolcott 2004).

10. Ethnography is flexible, adaptive. Well, if we can't seem to get ethnography to hold still, perhaps we can commend it for being flexible and adaptive. And indeed it is. From the ethnographer's perspective, that can be one of its finest features, allowing him or her to take advantage of whatever opportunities arise. Serendipity, we call it. (Recall the lesson of chapter 3.)

But so flexible and adaptive an approach can leave one in serious doubt as to how to proceed. It is not unknown among the ranks of anthropologists—the lesser known ones, I hasten to add—that some of them become so struck with the limitless possibilities of everything that could be studied that they never actually get around to studying anything at all. Even for those who thrive on the opportunities of whatever setting they find themselves in, to outsiders it is never quite clear what the ethnographer will come up with.

If you hire an ethnographer to conduct an ethnographic study without a specific assignment, or send a student off for a year of fieldwork without a firm objective in mind, you never know what to expect as a result. That makes both ethnographer and ethnography relatively unfettered. I have seen ethnography defined as "what ethnographers do." When you are beginning a study, that level of detail can prove remarkably unhelpful.

11. Ethnography is corroborative. One of ethnography's strengths is that we use multiple sources of data. The long-term nature of fieldwork adds immeasurably to the feeling that our accounts are reliable. We ourselves can be unaware of how those accounts are often dependent on few informants—perhaps only one or two individuals willing to talk at length and answer our myriad queries. Long-term periods of fieldwork are also liable to find us making use of fewer and fewer channels for gathering our data, thus narrowing rather than broadening our sources of information.

As desirable as triangulation seems when talked about in seminar, just how do you go about checking up on what your informants are telling you without creating tension, even rivalries, in the community where you conduct your study: "Who told you *that?*" We are at the mercy of our informants, although we are not anxious to admit to our vulnerability and not anxious to suggest the tenuousness of what we are able to report. It has been suggested that we ought to dwell more on the "confirmability" of what we have to say. You can overdo the tentativeness of an account, however, if you begin every statement with the reminder that you offer but one instance, at one particular point in time, and no generalizations are warranted.

In the end, it seems that readers themselves are left to assess the "truth value" of our accounts as *more-or-less* accurate on such qualities as "internal validity" that call not for everything to be "true" but for the plausibility of the overall account. As Paul Kutsche reminds novice anthropological fieldworkers, "Remember that you are constructing a model of a culture, not telling *the* truth about your data; there are numerous truths" (Kutsche 1998:96).

12. Ethnography is idiosyncratic and individualistic. Well, finally, a criterion that holds up rather well. But it hardly points the way except to state the obvious: in the long run, we are left to judge each effort on its own. There is no standard mold, no absolute way to assess all ethnographies. And what holds true today was true even "back then." Roger Sanjek reports that in 1927 Margaret Mead wanted to write a second, more scholarly monograph to complement the work she had just completed, *Coming of Age in Samoa*, which was aimed at a popular audience. Before beginning, Mead identified and read a handful of what we recognize today as ethnographic classics.

In Mead's own words, "I gathered together a pile of the famous monographs of the period ... and studied their arrangements." And what Mead discovered, as Sanjek reports, was that the "arrangements" in each of these works was unique: *"There was no single all-purpose model* to which her Samoa data could be affixed and a monograph result. Each author presented a mass of material, and each had designed an internal architecture upon which this mass was hung. These two properties—rich ethnographic detail and cohesive supporting framework—continue to animate the anthropological aesthetic." [Sanjek 1998:99.]

An "Adequate" List

Well, there you have it. After searching for ethnography's essence for much of my professional life, and making a concerted effort especially during the time I spent

CHARACTERISTICS OF ETHNOGRAPHY

- ❧ holistic
- ❧ cross-cultural
- ❧ comparative
- ❧ authentic
- ❧ real
- ❧ intimate
- ❧ non-judgmental
- ❧ descriptive
- ❧ specific
- ❧ adaptive
- ❧ corroborative
- ❧ idiosyncratic

preparing the first draft of *Ethnography: A Way of Seeing*, I had finally discovered for myself what Margaret Mead realized back in 1927: there is no single all-purpose definition of, or model for, ethnography. My criteria did not supply the firm guidelines that I had been looking for; they were broad indicators at best. Most of them were present most of the time; not a single one was absolutely essential.[2] The table opposite lists characteristics of ethnography that should be considered.

And One Thing More

Ethnographies traditionally have been—and as circumstances allow, continue to be—characterized as presented in the table. Yet not one of these attributes appears to be indispensable, and meeting every one of them does not insure that the end result will be ethnography. The ethnographer needs to have a feel for which among the attributes is appropriate for meeting intended purposes and to have a general idea of expectations and limits. It is how one's data are drawn together into a cohesive account that gets at the essence of ethnography. It is something the ethnographer does with the data, not exotic bits of data by themselves but how they are combined into a cohesive whole and shaped into a satisfactory—and identifiable—form. The secret lies in solid mindwork, as revealed in the final write up, not only a flair for fieldwork.

As anthropologist Ward Goodenough has explained, the anthropologist "attributes" culture, or social structure, to a group. Other social scientists working in related disciplines have their preferred concepts for making their accounts "cohere." They may make offhand references to "culture," just as ethnographers feel free to draw on the key concepts used by other social scientists (such as "institution" in sociology). But if the end product is to be ethnography, "culture" or some equivalent concept—such as social structure, worldview, or Jean Lave's interesting notion of "community of practice" (Lave 1991:29ff)—must be there. To analyze data drawn from such everyday sources, economists, historians, sociologists, and so on employ the concepts that both characterize and underwrite their particular disciplines and the work of their colleagues. Along with giving the familiar shapes or forms that we expect in different arenas of practice, those concepts make their efforts recognizable for what they are intended to be.

For the ethnographer—the American ethnographer, at least—those data are worked into a cohesive mass with the addition of the concept of culture. Culture is not "there," waiting demurely to be discovered, it is something the ethnographer adds (and must add) because that is how American ethnographers make their data workable. British ethnographers have traditionally achieved comparable results with social structure, which, of course, we don't feel works quite as well.

The basic "stuff" of ethnography is contained in myriad raw facts of observation, little kernels that we collect, sort through, and later combine with the help of culture to achieve our synthesis. Variety is inherent both in what we choose to collect and what we subsequently do with it. Like loaves of bread, no two ethnographies could ever be exactly the same. And because some ethnographies are well written and therefore are more satisfying, they are the ones we read.

That raises a necessary but separate point about the final project—ethnographies are a potent force only to the extent that they are read. A talented fieldworker can satisfy all the above criteria and still come up short, not because the fieldwork is inadequate, but because the writing does not reach an adequate standard. Myriad completed ethnographies languish on the shelves because no one finds them interesting enough to read.

There is no single term that I can identify to explain this, but perhaps the word "sparkle" is sufficiently mysterious and vague to point to what I am suggesting. Some ethnographies lack adequate sparkle to make them sufficiently satisfying for readers that we want to include them among the "classics" or at least note them among our personal favorites.

I have written a monograph on this topic, so I have added what I can to encourage fieldworkers to be diligent at their writing and to make them more self-conscious about it (Wolcott 2009). There is no secret to writing well, nor is being able to write well a matter in which serendipity can have a hand. I think that the real work comes about through editing, revising, rewriting. And then editing, revising, and rewriting some more. Do you have the stamina for it?

CHAPTER SIX
Ethics and Intimacy in Fieldwork

The criterion of intimacy in my list of customary attributes of ethnography has become more problematic for me over the years and seems to warrant special attention. Here I deal with the issue as fully as I can, pulling no punches, at the same time resisting the urge to sermonize. I base these reflections on personal experience, as I have done throughout the book.

How Long Is a Long-Term Relationship?

How long an acquaintanceship must be to qualify as "long-term" is a first question to ask, and it is largely ignored in discussions of fieldwork criteria, so this attribute is something of an abstraction. Even if we reach agreement that ethnographers are simply more intimate, their acquaintance more long term, than most other kinds of social research, we have a criterion that seems headed in the right direction, but is stated in such a way that a beginning fieldworker would hardly be able to tell whether criteria for a satisfactorily intimate relationship had been satisfied or not. Similarly, what exactly constitutes an "intimate" relationship? Again, my dictionary (American Heritage) provides definitions of the adjective *intimate* that go either way, on the one hand affirming that it means *involving a warm friendship,* on the other, as being in a *sexual relationship.* My experience extends over the full range.

Early Fieldwork

In my first fieldwork, it seemed to take forever to establish a reasonably close relationship with any villager. I was, after all, in a rather stereotyped and formal role as village teacher. It was evident from the first moments that some of the pupils in my class harbored the resentment they had felt toward their previous teacher, a man who was not cruel as much as totally incompetent in the classroom. As a consequence, they had a deep feeling of anger and resentment toward the school, and whoever was occupying it, that had been communicated even to the youngest village children. Less than an hour after arriving at the village I had only begun unpacking when I heard a strange noise outside the teacherage (the living quarters attached to a school, especially in rural areas). Rocks were being thrown at the building by two young preschoolers standing outside, a harbinger of the enthusiasm with which I was to be met. It took most of the year and all of my energy to keep the class—as many as twenty-eight pupils—sufficiently at task that we could get through a normal school day.

Village adults were friendly but reserved, remaining distant except when they had had a few beers, at which time they would suddenly warm toward me. It was not until school ended the following June and I joined as extra crew on the chief's purse seine fishing boat that I realized what friends they had become, and in spite of many difficulties of the year I felt genuinely sad at departing. Chief Henry Bell and his entire family were among my closest friends and supporters. At the close of the school year I heard him announce to a meeting of all adult villagers, "This year we had the best teacher we ever had."

In my next study, that of the elementary school principal, a comparable reserve seemed to prevail that I also attribute to the formality of educator roles. The principal was completely forthcoming in his every word and deed, yet I always felt he was making a conscious effort to be the *good Christian* he strived to be, rather than the straight shooter I hoped he might be. He was the epitome of the too-pleasant church greeter, an active role he fulfilled for his church but also a way of coping that he used to help guide him in his chosen career. But I would never fault him for his openness in talking about any issue or problem that he felt might be of interest to my study.

In Rhodesia the distance between Blacks and Whites permeated every interaction. Although we made friends among Whites we had no close friendships, and responsibilities for every bit of business relating to the beer gardens were conducted formally. We sensed a closeness among the long-term White population, but as overseas visitors there only for a short time we remained outsiders to it.

In the study of the change effort in the school district a number of educators (teachers mostly) were eager informants because they wanted to be sure that their side of the story was represented, but again roles were prescribed and there was no need to strive for intimacy when people felt free to discuss their perceptions of what was happening to them in their professional roles. I was surprised to learn of married couples who held various jobs or worked at different schools but failed to mention their personal relationships in talking about how the project affected them, as if informal networks made no difference at all.

Student Problems

During these years I was also mentoring students who were doing their doctoral research under my supervision. Although none of my students' ethical problems reached the level where it was necessary to involve the institution,[1] their problems caused some agony, and to this day one problem remains unresolved.

The first problem came about with a nursing student conducting fieldwork in a new neonatal care unit at a local hospital. At one point, she became quite concerned with the way the unit was operating, and since she was writing what was deemed "a report," the hospital somehow saw the possibility of an impending lawsuit and threatened to dismiss her study if she intended to be critical in her final account. I could not determine whether it was a case of censorship or simply unfamiliarity with the ethnographic approach, but my student decided to pull her punches and eased off on what she might have reported that was causing her critical stance. She was able to establish an uneasy truce. The student completed her dissertation, but also gained a perspective on how hospitals maintain a healthy image of their own.

In the second instance, my recently-arrived student from Korea insisted convincingly that she would be a truly naïve and objective observer in an American high school. In spite of enthusiastic support from the principal we were both confronted by the school superintendent with the question, "If you see anything going on that might cause concern for the administration, you would report it immediately, wouldn't you?" Both the student and I were dumbfounded by the question, since it would effectively make her a tool of the administration and thus an informer on student life, exactly the opposite of the role she intended to play. I must admit that I could not see our way out of that issue, and we both had to retreat until we could come up with a satisfactory answer. A level-headed colleague in education, Ray Hull, provided the straightforward answer we were too flummoxed to provide. He suggested that my student might respond that *of course* she would report anything that posed a *genuine threat* to the school, but she also could remind him that she was interested in the *customary and usual activities* at the school; she would not feel any obligation to report on these. She was allowed to conduct her study, and it turned out to be a superb study—without any incident that would have cast her in the informer role (see Chang 1982). The lesson here is that questions can occur any time researchers are too close to the situation to see their way out; others with cooler heads may prevail.

The third ethical problem remains unresolved to this day. It concerns a researcher who made a devil's bargain in order to conduct research she wanted to do, a study of a Mystery School. To get the permission of the school's director, she had to promise not to reveal any of the "mysteries" of the school. The study was completed in 1989. Today, twenty-one years later, it remains locked away, the researcher having kept her promise and the proprietor retaining full ownership of her mysteries. The researcher believed that the proprietor would relent over the years, for she told her story in an unthreatening and unrevealing way, but a promise is a promise. And there this awkward case rests.

To the Recent Past

Now to the recent past and to the present. Volumes concerning problems with sex and the fieldworker began appearing in the 1990s in books like *Taboo* (Kulick and Willson, 1995) and *Out In The Field* (Lewin and Leap, 1996). One wonders whether intimacy itself is ever desirable when the threat of possible discovery or betrayal lurks in every ethnographic report, revealing things told in confidence, or inadvertently reporting something that embarrasses the teller. We all live under the shadow of Matt Miles and Mike Huberman's telling quote, "Fundamentally, field research is an act of betrayal, no matter how well intentioned or well integrated the researcher" (Miles and Huberman 1984:233).

As I wrote in the previous chapter, length of time in the field can, indeed, become a two edged sword: duration of stay is no guarantee of better fieldwork. The longer one stays, the greater chance to screw up the relationship, antagonize someone, or take a giant misstep. Mistrust is far easier to achieve than trust. Because we are there to gather information, most of us can act our best selves, at least for awhile. But the longer we stay, the less likely we are to be able to keep up a front and remain consistent in our own role playing. And as human beings, we are likely to begin spending more time among those with whom we feel comfortable.

Now turn that situation around: what if, under your constant watch for how serendipity may be working on your behalf, you discover that an informant has unexpectedly appeared before you. Paragon of Virtue that I attempted to be during my earlier days of fieldwork, things got completely turned around in my final study, *Sneaky Kid and Its Aftermath: Ethics and Intimacy in Fieldwork*. The conditions under which I ordinarily work changed dramatically when I asked someone to be an informant *after* we had become sexually involved.

A year earlier this young man, whom I introduced as Brad or the "Sneaky Kid," in chapter 4, had begun living on a remote part of the hilly slope on which my home resides. He had hastily constructed a cabin in the belief that he was on city parkland adjoining mine.

It took me awhile to locate him after a neighbor's son reported meeting him while walking in the woods. I was not too happy with the idea of having a squatter living on my place, but I reasoned I could allow him to stay, for I did not think it likely he would remain long. I did not realize how determined he was to learn how to survive on his own, but he ended up staying a remarkable two years. Initially, getting to know him was slow work, but occasionally I needed help around my place, and I knew he needed incidental cash to buy things that he could not scrounge or steal outright.

In time we became well acquainted. I greatly admired his determination to make the best of the situation: to establish a life for himself, with no income other than food stamps, no contact with family (although his father, from whom he was estranged, lived in town, and I made it possible for his mother to reach him by telephone at my house), and no friends. He had dwelt on my place for about a year before we became sexually involved. As I got to know him better and had grown rather fond of him I realized that his story might be of interest to others, especially anyone who shared my interest in the process of enculturation without the full benefit of formal education. To my surprise he agreed to let me tape the story of his life, for as he boasted, he had experienced more than many lads his age: "I've definitely had more experiences than some of the people I went to school with, and I've had my ears opened more than they have. In *some* things, I'm wiser than other kids my age" (Wolcott 1983:19).

He estimated that it would take about twelve hours to relate his story. We agreed that I would not reveal anything that he felt too personal, most certainly including the nature of our relationship. As I reported, those twelve hours winnowed to twelve minutes once he began his account, but with patience on my part he was able to his fill in with details and anecdotes. When I finally had his rambling account organized around what appeared to me to be some dominant themes in his life, I asked him to read what I had written to see if I had it right and had not included anything he preferred to keep to himself. (Sexual matters were strictly personal, but I was surprised at his lack of concern revealing petty thefts and even an attempted robbery.)

Toward the end of his second year he began showing signs of strange behavior and began complaining that he felt a constant "sledge hammer to the brain." With considerable urging I was able to get him to a mental health counselor, but he was not satisfied with the suggestion that he might do well in an institution, although that alternative had some attractive features compared with what he was willing to admit was his hard life. When the military would not accept him because he had not completed grade ten, he expressed a sense that things were becoming hopeless.

We had built our relationship slowly. But we had time to nurture and develop it before he decided to move on, and in that time I felt we had become quite close. I was *distraught* (in my dictionary's sense of being deeply agitated from emotional conflict) at the idea of his leaving. I knew he had no idea of where he would go or what he would do next. He, too, seemed to have become *distraught* (in the dictionary's sense of being mad or insane) worrying about his future.

I now understand that he was sinking into schizophrenia (for that he was right on schedule, according to the American Psychiatric Association's DSM III, with a mental illness that often strikes young men at about his age), for both Norman and I had begun to notice a radical change in behavior in his final weeks at the cabin. After he departed, I did not see or hear from him for the next two and a half years, although when he left he promised to keep in touch. I actually expected him to return any day and to reinvigorate the life he had been able to create for himself.

What a surprise to have him return unannounced two and a half years later in a wild rage and to have him threaten Norman and me, set fire to our house and burn it completely to the ground, totally destroying both the house and our every belonging.

You can make of it what you want—perhaps it really was the nature of our relationship that resulted in his acting as he did, but there are myriad other possibilities to consider, and not all of them can be linked to the ethics of the situation. He had departed as a highly disturbed youth, and we could find no way to halt his descent into a depressed state. We learned that after a couple of months of hustling (for sex) on the streets, he arrived at his mother's home in Southern California, where she immediately had him placed under psychiatric care.

All I have been able to learn more recently is that he has mellowed, but he seemingly maintains his deep resentment toward me. I continue to hold him responsible for the biggest betrayal of my life, but I am not sure I can hold him personally responsible for something that may have been out of his control.

Matter of fact, I am not absolutely certain of anything concerned with these events (see Wolcott 2010). I do know that it took me a long time to get things into perspective, and longer still to recognize that even in the face of personal catastrophe, serendipity was standing by, ready to turn the events into an account meaningful and worthy of critical attention. Even if the events did involve me personally!

Looking Back

My previous experience with ethics pales by comparison with the story of Sneaky Kid, although these events posed only milder forms of issues similar to those I have faced elsewhere. In all my studies I have had to face the question of what to reveal, what to keep to myself. In the Sneaky Kid case, I promised at the outset that I would not reveal anything too personal. And to that end I had him review what I had written.

Until I began the earlier project that resulted in *Teachers Vs. Technocrats*, where I was working among my own colleagues and became so disheartened at the unrest some of them were foisting on and for the school district, I had a relatively easy time with ethics.

Among the Kwakiutl my biggest decision had to do with whether to mask the name of the village, and I did so largely to satisfy myself that the identity of everyone in the village was protected. But long afterward I realized that only a handful of people in the entire world had any idea who the villagers were or would really be concerned, and the people involved would know who was who anyway, so what I had done was effectively set "my" village adrift in the sea of otherwise carefully specified villages, and gained little by doing so. Merely changing a few names might have accomplished my purposes.

I have now experienced what I consider unethical behavior of educators who probably consider themselves to be super ethical. Two educators at a college in the northeast had a personal problem with my ethics and felt it their duty to berate me for having told what they considered to be only half a story (the part that I was authorized to tell in the original Sneaky Kid account, in Wolcott 1983). My interlopers did not stop with expressing their disappointment, they shared their concern with a professional organization that was planning to reprint my first article about the Sneaky Kid in a manual for researchers. The editor of that publication (the late Richard Jaeger) defended the article and allowed it to remain with the other entries after seeking an opinion from three scholars asked to render independent judgments. (To my surprise, my work received approval from only two of them—nevertheless that constituted a majority.)

But that did not stop my detractors, who next set out to unmask the identity of Sneaky Kid himself, presumably in the hope that they could build the case against me. By what series of technological machinations they were able to discover who he was and where he lives is beyond me— not even my publisher knows Sneaky Kid's real name, and although I know the city in which he resides I have never obtained his address. But my two interlopers have certainly impressed upon me both the impossibility of absolutely protecting anonymity and the lengths some people will go to try to find out what they do not need to know.

Their behavior has reinforced my feeling that ethics is as likely to become a negative force as a positive one, something one can draw on to find fault with others. One is never commended for "good" ethics: "bad" ethics seem to draw attention only after the fact. I recognize efforts to alert the rest of us to how far others have gone to tell us how we ought to behave (see Fleuhr-Lobban's excellent account, 2003), but I strongly suspect such accounts preach to the choir. As long as we make finding out about others our mission, there will be ethical issues for us to resolve whenever we find out more than we were supposed to.

I have lost faith in the politics of acting ethically. Since I began fieldwork, I have always taken responsibility for my own behavior in the field and in what I later report. But I am not so sure that ours is an ethical line of work—in the course of finding out everything we want to know, we can't help finding out things we do not want, or need, to know.

A Responsible Ethics

The responsibility for what we reveal remains, as it must, only with ourselves. Talking about ethics is a great way to keep everyone busy without having to change anything. In my reading, it strikes me that anthropologists lost their way when the term *responsibility* disappeared from their discourse. Hear the original words of the American Anthropological Association's Code of Ethics drafted in 1971 under what were then labeled the first Principles of Professional Responsibility: " In research, anthropologists' paramount responsibility is to those they study" (Fleuhr-Lobban 2003:xii).

Through the years that idea has been compromised by problems with secret research, undercover research, clandestine research, covert inquiry, counterinsurgency— we have a lot of names for research that some find unethical. Anthropologist Gerald Berreman, principal author of the original "Principles of Professional Responsibility," says he still prefers the epilogue to the PPR, not just because he wrote it, but as a reasonable statement of ethical requirements:

> In the final analysis, anthropological research is a human undertaking, dependent upon choices for which the individual bears ethical as well as scientific responsibility. That responsibility is a human, not superhuman, responsibility. To err is human, to forgive humane. This statement of Principles of Professional Responsibility is not designed to punish, but to provide guidelines which can minimize the occasions upon which there is a need to forgive. [Gerald Berreman, quoted in Fleuhr-Lobban. 2003:77-78.]

Anyone who has ever taught qualitative methods realizes that it would be absolutely impossible to script out every possible encounter that a student might have in the field, and thus it is impossible to anticipate all the ethical dilemmas that students may face. The best we can do is talk in a useful, constructive way about ethical issues and try to prevent students from taking unnecessary risks. I think a risk-benefit assessment is a worthwhile exercise, where the benefits that may be derived are weighed against the probable costs of obtaining such information. But ethics are always a matter of judgment, and judgments are always in flux. Over the years I think I have grown fonder of transparency as a way of handling truth.

I have told the truth. But I have not told everything, even about myself. I am silent about some things, but what I have told is true. I am guided by an old proverb that reminds us that if you tell the truth you don't have to try to remember what you told them the last time! For me, that is about as close as I can come to defining the real lesson of ethics.[2]

CHAPTER SEVEN
Education by Analogy

These "lessons" are drawing to a close, but I have one final idea to share with you. It is something that I have been meaning to write about: the use of analogy in writing. This reveals the teacher in me, the part that wants to make sure that the lesson has been understood. One looks for analogies intended to help others understand. The intent is never to make things more complex, but to make comparison with something presumed to be familiar or more readily understood.

You realize from this account that my interests are primarily in the field of anthropology and education. Through the years that I have been writing, I have often made use of analogy. You can do the same, especially whenever you feel you may not have succeeded in making your ideas as clear as you intended. Most certainly ours is not rocket science; we want our audiences to understand what we have to say, and sometimes an analogy can help.

Riding on a Boat

One of the first analogies I drew on is to taking a boat ride. I pictured the Indian children in my classroom as though they were passengers on a boat, and in Kwakiutl country with its many island villages, everyone spent a lot of time doing just that. On a boat there isn't much for passengers to do except to sit and wait until it reaches its destination, and that is what my pupils seemed to be doing, sitting there waiting for the boat—or in this case, the school year—to reach the end of its journey, when everyone could get off. They did become more responsive as the year went on, but there were many times that I had the feeling they so ably communicated—just sit and be patient until it's over.

Doing the principal study, I had occasion to think about the boat analogy again, this time from the skipper's perspective. I thought of the principal as embarking on a yearly cruise, with his crew of teachers signed on without opportunity to replace any of them until the journey's end. Passengers come and go at each port of call along the way, but until the voyage is over there is no chance to sign on new crew or to replace members who are unsatisfactory. That seemed to be the way principals talked, always with a look to the future ("next year's sailing") when things would be far better and a more carefully selected crew in place.

Commercial Fertilizer

My search for an analogy to use in *Transforming Qualitative Data: Description, Analysis and Interpretation* (Wolcott, 1994) was for a mix consisting essentially of three main parts, any one of which may dominate the other two. The critical decision about what proportion to include of each ingredient is determined by the intended purpose of the study: whether in this case to describe, to analyze, or to interpret. Of course, should a researcher strive to attain all three outcomes at once, equal amounts would have to be included of the three components, but I wanted to emphasize that attending to any one of the three, or at most to some combination of analysis or interpretation coupled with a strong descriptive component, is customary and adequate. We don't expect qualitative reports to try to achieve all three outcomes equally or to present the perfectly rounded study.

The analogy that came to mind was to commercial fertilizer, the one comprised of three essential components and abbreviated N-P-K. Those symbols stand, respectively, for three essential ingredients: elemental Nitrogen, anhydride of Phosphoric Acid, and soluble potash (chemical symbol "K" from *kalium*).

With plants, whether one's purpose is to enhance lush, fast growth; to stimulate flower or seed production; or to build overall strength, especially in roots and branches, one chooses the fertilizer with the particular ratio of ingredients N, P and K to achieve the desired results. The analogy to possible outcomes for handling data was to suggest that one applies the chemical fertilizer appropriate for one's purposes. One might wish to accomplish all three objectives (as with a composite 16-16-16), but that probably indicates the absence of a well-defined purpose, an effort to achieve whatever outcome one can get, or, as likely, someone who doesn't know exactly what he wants. My point was that of the three possible emphases in qualitative research, one should recognize what he or she is trying to achieve and invest efforts to that end, rather than try to achieve every possible outcome with every study.

I did not mean to disparage any of the three. If you do intend to produce a basically descriptive study, you invest most heavily in that effort and therefore can minimize analysis and interpretation. If you want the results to speak for themselves, you invest more in analysis, because analysis suggests that you have followed a strict observance of accepted, standardized procedures. And if an interpretive mode suits, you focus on efforts to offer plausible explanation to accompany the descriptive account. You need to recognize what you are trying to achieve (and why not focus on what you do best?).

There are always other trace ingredients in commercial fertilizer—elements such as calcium, magnesium, copper and the like, just as there are trace qualities (e.g. compassion, humor, suspense) in any qualitative study. The analogy allows for them.

If you are comfortable with and talented in using statistical procedures, you couple your description with analysis and thus attempt to bridge the seeming gap that has grown between qualitative and quantitative approaches. But for starters, I usually recommend writing an intensely descriptive study, and topping it off with a modest effort at interpretation. Don't be shy about presenting a study consisting essentially of solid description—that is still our forte!

My only problem was to reassure readers that my analogy to fertilizer was not a subtle reflection on the product itself.

Drawing House Plans

In thinking about the basic issue of organizing one's data and presenting an ethnographic account, an analogy that came to mind was to the many options we have for designing a house. You can borrow the house plans of an already constructed house that you like, and of course there is nothing to prevent you from using a mirror image or positioning a house differently on a site to maximize a view, an approach, winter light, traffic noise, etc. Or you can use a plan from any of the numerous books filled with house plans.

But choosing a ready-made design is not the only option for building. Another alternative is to start from scratch, either designing as you go or incorporating desirable features from several houses. One might also plan and build a house one section at a time, in modular fashion. Too, there is always the alternative of buying something ready-made, either a mobile home or a manufactured one. There are many possible ways to find the house one has in mind.

So, too, with finding a way to structure one's study—there are multiple ways to go about it, and many possible plans available for the neophyte who does not want to construct something completely on his or her own. For each of the social sciences there are a host of general texts that reveal how some author has organized that academic field, and most of these books offer a plan that can be used to organize a new study. That is the way that I used Felix Keesing's book (described in chapter 1) to identify organizing categories for my Kwakiutl study. It also may be possible to find a book with a table of contents approximating what one has in mind and to adapt it for one's own purposes, either in part or in toto. The possibilities seem unlimited.

Baking a Loaf of Bread

I really felt a sense of satisfaction when I found a good analogy to the process of doing ethnography. In preparing *Ethnography: A Way of Seeing* I felt that finding a working analogy would be especially helpful. Following the lesson of the previous chapter, I realized that I needed to find something that did not have a single *essential* ingredient, but that appeared to have a number of customary ones. I saw a possibility in an analogy to breadmaking, especially when I discovered that not even wheat flour is an essential element. [Flour made from starchy seeds that are technically not grass seeds can be used in its place.]

I had fun finding parallels: from choosing among polished vs. coarse-ground "kernels" of data, to punching down the rising dough so there won't be any holes in it. Recognize, too, that once the loaf goes into the oven (or a study goes to the printer) it is too late to make any changes. We must be content with the finished product, and we can only hope that what we have created is not only pleasing to a broad audience but acceptable to our most discriminating patrons.

How the flour is combined into a mixture, and what is added that allows the ingredients to form into a workable mass, all seemed to be accounted for in the analogy. Furthermore, I saw a parallel in that some bakers prefer flour that comes from grains that they themselves collect. Whether they want that flour to be refined or stone-ground also has a familiar ring among ethnographers who must determine the form they want their data to be in before they work with it, and what, if anything, is to be added by way of improvers. Like some bakers, some ethnographers prefer to work with highly refined material (the "closet quantifiers," as I like to think of them). Other ethnographers, like other bakers, insist that the ingredients they use be as close to the natural state as possible.

Whatever the case, there must be a liquid of some kind to allow dry ingredients to mix and form a workable mass. For me, that was the critical test of the analogy—the fact that the baker, like the ethnographer, must add something (liquid for the baker, culture for the ethnographer) in order to work up the material, which is then shaped to look more-or-less like the loaves one's colleagues bake.

The last step, is, of course, the baking and distribution (read: printing and marketing) of the final product.

I was pleased when the analogy led to another thought: the idea that with proper instruction almost anyone can bake a loaf of bread. One does not have to be formally trained as an ethnographer to come up with ethnography, any more than one needs to be trained as a baker to bake a loaf of bread. Students do it all the time! But one does need a clear idea of the customary ingredients, the possible substitutions, the improvers, the acceptable range of variation, and so forth, as well as a clear idea of how the end product will look, and where and how it is to be served.

The ingredients themselves are not that special. As Geertz observes of the "ingredients" of ethnography, it is not their origins that recommend them (1968:vii). Rather, they are ordinary, everyday materials, collected in ordinary everyday ways. That is another distinguishing characteristic of most ethnographies: they are not accounts of heroic individuals performing heroic feats, but of quite ordinary folk going about their everyday affairs.

It is how the raw material is used that turns some accounts into ethnography, while other accounts become myths, biography, and so forth, or are turned into products characteristic of other social sciences or arenas of practice. It is what someone does with the explicit intent of producing ethnography that makes ethnography out of some accounts and not of others. And that is why, working with the same basic materials, ethnographers end up with their particular product while social scientists of different persuasions end up with slightly different interpretations.

I stress that the ethnographer adds something that makes a study ethnographic, the symbolic interactionist or phenomenologist or feminist researcher in each case adds something different to come up with a slightly different result. These accounts are variously seasoned with compassion, humor, suspense, those trace elements mentioned earlier, to satisfy the traditions and tastes of their various audiences.

The final judgment is reserved for the finished product. There are bakers or ethnographers (like me) who tend to stick to the old ways, to follow the tried and true recipes, the standard treatment. Others like to experiment or push the limits. Often the lines are drawn between generations. Old timers are likely to become fixed in their ways and to decry any new-fangled technologies that seem to ignore the character-building qualities associated with traditional ways—such as bread-making machines that can do the sticky work, or computer programs that speed up the tedious processing of data (but who said it was tedious?).

One never knows if an analogy really works. As pleased as I was with this one, I do not recall anyone singling it out or commending its appropriateness. Maybe I pushed too hard; I was having fun discovering features common to breadmaking and the making of ethnography. Perhaps it worked and no one thought to tell me.

The Moiety Analogy

Baking a loaf of bread is not, of course, the same as doing an ethnography, but the analogy seemed to fit. When I hit upon the moiety idea, from traditional anthropology, I began to wonder if I was observing a genuine moiety form of social organization. I guess I tipped my hand, for by the time readers reached the end of the book, some of them felt I had presented the case as though the teachers and technocrats really were moieties. I even admit to

beginning to feel that way myself—everything fit together so well.

So what is one to do when the analogy seems perfect?
I guess at the end of your account you might let a little air
out of any analogy just as you might let a little air out of
an over inflated tire or balloon, to ensure that your reader
understands, that you understand, that you are working
with an analogy, and that the essence of analogy is the
likeness of only some parts. I think my readers would
have been more comfortable had I inventoried more ways
that teachers and technocrats did *not* meet every attribute
of a moiety form of social organization.

One such critic wrote in a letter received at the Center
in November 1977 (the Center was the publisher of the book):

> The review of moiety concepts is an interesting academic
> exercise, as is the effort to achieve a "moiety-like" fit with
> the data. Many people will be attracted by this; it may
> well lead to glib acquisition of a new term in educational
> jargon. Wolcott's disclaimers of intent to demonstrate
> actual moiety existence are both modest and protective,
> but are ineffectual because of his exclusive uses of data
> and his own repeated use of "moiety" as a firmly demon-
> strated fact (the ultimate on p. 244: "... members of *the
> two moieties identified in the case study* ... created their
> own hell... .)" [Italics added.]

It was a valid criticism. The book did seem to pro-
voke responses from readers, a number of whom were
graduate students in classes with titles like "Schools as
Organizations." A colleague who was teaching such a class
sent me a poem one of his students wrote in response to
the assignment to write a critique of the book. I quote here
only the final stanzas of a much longer poem:[1]

Part III is the heart of the book
Where Wolcott continues to look
For cultural ties
(Ethnographically wise)
That exist in school cranny and nook.

Interactions that he numbers four
Are at the moiety core.
Most of these are OK,
Some connections are, basically, poor. [Ouch!]

Two samples come quickly to view:
"Decoration"—and "sacredness," too –
Who cares who's best dressed?
Or who has what crest?
He's reaching, and I say: POOH-POOH!

The section I liked best of all,
Had to do with the "push" and the "stall":
Exchange, rivalry
These "lit up" for me,
Compliance, resistance, et al.!

A word 'bout cohesion comes last
Alignment of all to hold fast.
"United we stand (within "ed biz" land)
So lay people cannot get past!

In summary (Thank God, you say?)
The reading was current—"today."
This unique point of view
(Once Part I was plowed through)
Blew the whistle on "ed games" we play.

I have continued my search for analogies and use them whenever I can. I tend to be a bit more cautious these days, having seen the criticism that some of the analogies that

I particularly favored were subjected to. Yet even when imperfect, analogies serve a useful function, if only by getting others to see what is wrong with them. You may have noticed, however, that while I have gotten older, my analogies have not been getting any better. So the lesson is to critique carefully those you intend to use, and use caution—you are making comparisons between things that by definition are *only* similar, not alike.

I thought you might be interested in what Spindler had to say about my analogy to moieties. I always kept in close touch with him, and whenever I had prepared something that I hoped he would find interesting, I sent him a copy. *Teachers versus Technocrats* was to that time my most ambitious effort to draw upon the anthropological literature, and I made sure he received a copy. I think I knew Spindler well enough to recognize that he had read as much about my use of the moiety concept as he intended to ("I just got started with it when I lost it"). I received this comment in a longer letter sent overseas while I was on my second sabbatical (May 1978). He wrote:

> Harry, your book is monumental, but I just got started with it when I lost it. It'll turn up. My first impression was that the moiety idea was not inappropriately used but that it was, perhaps, not entirely necessary, excepting as a kind of introductory metaphor. This is *not* a comment on the analysis itself, which is *excellent*.

❧ ❧ ❧

Do the lessons ever stop...

CHAPTER EIGHT
Lessons End

On the other hand (I can hear an alert copy editor wondering where the first hand was), maybe I should have labeled this as a *pri'mer* after all. It has turned out to be more like an undercoat, something that prepares a surface for the finish coat to follow. Supplying that finish coat will be up to you. If I have achieved anything here it has been only to help you understand ethnography a little better, recognize some things to watch for, and be aware of what I think you will have to do to be sure that you are really doing ethnography (assuming, of course, that is what you have set out to do). Note that the educator part of me already thinks he knows what you need to know in order to do that.

To me, the first lesson about ethnography is the one I placed first: that it is about something that you have personally tried to know and to understand rather well. And something that you believe others will want to know about, at least as seen through your eyes and from direct experience. Something like a Kwakiutl village and school in the academic year 1962–1963, or the beer gardens of Bulawayo in 1970, or a Sneaky Kid in 1981. You get to select what you read about, but if you choose one of these topics, you expect an ethnography that deals with it to be holistic, authentic, as intimate as seems necessary for the case at hand, and because there is a human presenting the account, you expect it to be somewhat idiosyncratic but you insist that it be truthful.

There were some corollaries accompanying that first lesson, including a smashing one about never feeling you have to defend your study of a single case, because, as Margaret Mead expressed it, each of us is "a perfect example, an organic representation of his complete cultural experience" (Mead 1953: 655), and none of us could possibly be more. And there were some ideas about looking for *themes* as a way to consolidate your observations and aggregate them into bigger units that begin to point the way to the ethos of a culture.

There were also some ideas about names, particularly about not feeling that everyone in a study needs to have a name that you create. There are so many other ways that you can use to identify individuals in a non-fictional account, such as the rank order that I used in the principal study. Above all, don't give your actors or your books names that people cannot pronounce. Leave that for the Greek tragedies (Aegisthus or Iphigenia or Aeschylus, indeed), and don't forget to translate foreign phrases or idioms, on the off chance that not everyone has studied the same foreign languages that you studied.

In the lesson of the third chapter, I tried simultaneously to console and to warn you about *time,* our truly independent variable. Like serendipity, it depends in part how you look at it, but in ethnographic work it is hard to think of time as an ally under any circumstances. In the field, you cannot escape the feeling that there will never be enough time when so much is happening (and if it isn't happening, you aren't paying sufficient attention). Once your fieldwork is completed, time will continue to run out on you, partly because you recognize the enormity of the task facing you but mostly because your thoughts don't seem to be coming together as you hoped and assumed they would. My counsel on that issue may not be very comforting: be patient and don't be too hard on yourself. It is absolutely impossible to rush a (satisfactory) conclusion. Say what you are able to say, and keep on mulling until you reach a stronger ending. I admitted to a quarter of a century lapse with my dissertation study before I had the kind of conclusion that I wanted. I failed to acknowledge the corresponding elation I felt when I knew that for me I had finally gotten it right. Was the wait worth it? Well, who I was waiting for to tell me that it was?

Serendipity's lesson is also something of a mixed message. It does not actually promise that things always work out, but it suggests that if you look at things in a positive way, you can usually find a silver lining somewhere. That can be another agonizingly slow process, and you might begin to wonder how many quarter-centuries each of us is allowed. I think such an approach misses the real message of serendipity, which is to appreciate however things happen to fall into place. Maybe each of us gets to meet only one Hugh Ashton or one Fraser-Ross in a lifetime, but if your lament is that you *never* have had a lucky break, it might be time to review your personal accounting system.

The lesson about organizing your account is simply that there is no one best way. In the years that I have been preaching this position I hope that I have not put graduate students at risk in claiming that this idea even holds for dissertation writing. Allow me one last story. One of the saddest days of my life was when as a guest lecturer I was describing my completed principal study to a group of foreign students. I had taken pains to fill my audience in on the details of why my first chapter was called, "A Principal Investigator in Search of a Principal." I hoped they would pick up on the sense of story that I was trying to convey and would offer something along the lines of my second chapter, which was actually titled "The Principal as a Person." But to my query, "Now, what do you think chapter 2 was about?" came only one word, chanted in unison, "Method." Like most graduate students everywhere, they had a fixed notion of how a research study is put together, and nothing could get in the way.

I concur that if you do not have a single creative bone in your body, your chapter 2 can look like almost everyone else's chapter 2, and your whole dissertation can follow the well worn formula I-H-M-R-D (introduction, hypothesis, methods, results, discussion), but who, other than possibly some die-hard committee member, would ever hold you to a rigid formula like that, especially if you are writing ethnography? My answer: if you are allowed, try telling your story your way. And if you are not allowed, tell it your way when you find the next opportunity to tell your story (which you must do if your study points to something that you feel is worthy and important).

You are welcome to join in the search for ethnography's essence, but I trust you will find the search itself worthwhile, for you will never succeed in finding the one-list-fits-all solution. Yet I commend the journey, for it can uncover a multitude of beliefs, hopes, dreams, and, of course, realities, for ethnography. It has long been apparent that ethnography itself is not sitting idly by waiting to be defined; it is constantly expanding and evolving to meet new insights and changing circumstances. And who knows, you may be able to offer a crisper distinction between how ethnographies can be both *authentic* and *real,* or *specific* and *idiosyncratic,* than I have been able to come up with.

Intimacy remains your responsibility and is therefore an issue that I must leave to you, for I do not know how one individual can supply an adequate answer for another. Sometimes by example, and not always too subtlely, I have tried to urge and cajole other ethnographers to reveal more of themselves in their writing, but I am not always sure what that would get them. To me, intimacy implies something sexual in nature, so I see it as a problem more often backed away from when it is not made explicit. It has always seemed incredible to me that so little of human passion is revealed in most ethnographies (there are exceptions), and I attribute that to a general apprehension shared among those who do this kind of work. I think this may have been the hope behind early advice that we can be neutral without having to be objective, but was that only fooling ourselves with another layer of masks?

One starting place is to develop some kind of personal standard for just how intimate one intends to be or to become in a particular study. At one time I set some criteria that I could use to define intimacy for my own purposes (Wolcott 1995:78–83). I decided that I would consider myself as having sufficient intimate knowledge of another person (for ethnographic purposes) if I knew: 1. An individual's sleeping arrangements, which, with refinement, became "Who sleeps by whom?"; 2. How that individual's laundry gets washed, dried, and put away; and 3. Something about his or her grandparents (Wolcott 1995:78–83). In contrast to the first two criteria, the third one insures only that we have talked of family or have shared stories revealing of family history. Although none of my criteria was very rigorous, I still was able only to *infer* about either of the first two in any of my earlier studies. Then, with Sneaky Kid, I met all the criteria head on, yet they did not even come close to the intimacy we shared. The lesson is clear, but for each of us the resolution is an individual responsibility. Only, you should have no regrets afterward. I don't.

As for analogies, once again I leave it up to you. Did the one I used here work? Prim'er or pri'mer? Or both? It's up to you.

Finally, let me underscore that ethnography's most important contribution is in purposeful and thorough description. That is what ethnographers do and that is how they continue to develop the ethnographic potential. Don't be cowed by the idea that we only describe—our contribution comes as well out of what we assess as being worthy of our descriptive effort. If description is something you do well, consider that a gift. If you are not good at it, work to enhance your capabilities. In that regard, I hope these lessons have helped. In future endeavors, think carefully about how and where you should direct your gaze, and then follow through with your most provocative analysis or interpretation.

NOTES

Chapter 1

1. This may have been the earliest use of the term "shadow" or "shadowing" that became popular in educational research ("shadow studies") and now appear everywhere. The term is not original, however; when I was growing up there was a nightly serial on the radio called "The Shadow."

2. Spindler's handwriting was always difficult to read. Sometimes when I knew I would be meeting with him, I brought along something he had written and asked him to "translate." Unless he could remember what he had intended, he was often at a loss himself. The comments quoted here are substantially what he wrote, or what I made of them at the time.

3. Barker's study, done with the help of others, was to record and report on the activity of every waking minute of one boy's (school) day. It was a remarkable behavioral study at the time, especially for psychologists.

4. My person-centered studies are the principal study referred to here and in *Sneaky Kid and Its Aftermath: Ethics and Intimacy in Fieldwork* (Wolcott 2002). My focus in the present paper is on the deliberations and events of one group, the Principal Selection Committee.

5. Subsequently I developed a talk that I could present when invited to speak to principals, but I was not always convinced they saw any humor in my title, "Spare Change," which did not end with a question mark.

6. My citations ran about two to one in favor of anthropologists, but I felt free to use whatever sources or concepts seemed relevant. Spindler was more conscious of developing the field of "anthropology and education" than I was at the time.

Chapter 2

1. This is the value of the subsequent revising and rewriting that Carolyn Ellis discusses in *Revision,* reminding us that we do well to recognize that our stories are "always partial, incomplete and full of silences, and told at a particular time, for a particular purpose, to a particular audience" (2009:13).

Chapter 3

1. At the time, the Korean Conflict.
2. Efforts continue to abound to change the name Kwakiutl. The effort is well intended, for the name Kwakiutl belongs rightfully to only one tribe among a widely dispersed people living along the British Columbia coast. However, I am skeptical that the effort will succeed, given the long duration (about 125 years) that the people have been known primarily by the name Kwakitul, or as Kwakwala-speakers. (For a discussion, see Macnair 1986.)

Chapter 4

1. I trust you recognize the subhead above as the title of my dissertation, not of the published book.

Chapter 5

1. My friend anthropologist Doug Foley once admonished, "I'll never understand your perverse, incessant desire to become 'more anthropological.' Despite all the good cultural analysis and description you always seem a bit preoccupied with that issue. Perhaps some day you will explain it all to me." (Letter to HW written August, 29, 1996.)

2. Don't let my terms or the number of them beguile you here—these words sometimes overlap in meaning, and there most certainly can be more or less than the twelve that I have chosen to adequately define the essence of ethnography. Borrow from my list to develop your own. It seems to me the task requires a minimum of five descriptors, but for me it took twelve.

Chapter 6

1. I had no unfavorable personal experience with IRBs (Institutional Review Boards). My general advice to students is to treat them the same way we obtain a driver's license—just give them what they ask for. I have never regarded them as ethical.

2. For further discussion about researching ethically, see Ellis 2009, especially pages 308–318. See also Kaler and Beres 2010: 91–106.

Chapter 7

1. Permission was granted by Leslie Lawson to quote from her limerick, originally submitted in fulfillment of an assignment prepared for a seminar "Schools as Organizations" in 1978. My appreciation is also extended to Professor Robert Everhart, who was able to track the address of his former student thirty-two years later.

REFERENCES AND
FURTHER READING

Agar, Michael H.
  1980 The Professional Stranger. Orlando, FL: Academic Press.
  1996 The Professional Stranger. 2nd ed. San Diego, CA:
    Academic Press.

American Psychiatric Association
  1980 Diagnostic and Statistical Manual of Mental Disorders III,
    Washington, DC: The Association.

Ashton, Hugh
  1952 The Basuto. London: Oxford University Press.

Barker, Roger G., and Herbert F. Wright
  1951 One Boy's Day: A Specimen Record of Behavior. New
    York: Harper. [Republished 1966 by Archon Books:
    Hamden, CT.]

Becker, Howard S.
  2007 Telling About Society. Chicago: University of Chicago
    Press.

Beer, C. G.
  1973 A View of Birds. In Minnesota Symposia of Child
    Psychology, Vol 7. Anne Pick, ed. Pp. 47–53. Minneapolis:
    University of Minnesota.

Benedict, Ruth
  1934 Patterns of Culture. Boston: Houghton, Mifflin.

Bernard, H. Russell, and Gery W. Ryan
  2010 Analyzing Qualitative Data: Systematic Approaches.
    Thousand Oaks, CA: Sage.

Bohannan, Paul
  1995 How Culture Works. New York: Free Press.

Chang, Heewon
  1982 Adolescent Life and Ethos: An Ethnography of a US High
    School. Washington, DC: Falmer Press.
Clifford, James
  1988 The Predicament of Culture. Cambridge, MA: Harvard
    University Press.
  1997 Spatial Practices: Fieldwork, Travel, and the Disciplining
    of Anthropology. *In* Anthropological Locations, Akhil Gupta
    and James Ferguson, eds. Pp. 185–222. Berkeley, CA:
    University of California Press.
Creswell, John W.
  1998 Qualitative Inquiry and Research Design: Choosing
    Among Five Traditions. Thousand Oaks, CA: Sage.
Dreeben, Robert
  1968 On What Is Learned in School. Reading, MA: Addison-
    Wesley Publishing Company.
Ellis, Carolyn
  2009 Revision: Autoethnographic Reflections on Life and Work.
    Walnut Creek, CA: Left Coast Press, Inc.
Evans-Pritchard, E. E.
  1940 The Nuer. London: Oxford University Press.
Fleuhr-Lobban, Carolyn, ed.
  2003 Ethics and the Profession of Anthropology, 2nd ed. Walnut
    Creek, CA: AltaMira Press.
Fox, Richard G.
  1991 Introduction. *In* Recapturing Anthropology: Working in
    the Present. Richard G. Fox, ed. Pp. 1–16. Santa Fe, NM:
    School of American Research Press.
Geertz, Clifford
  1968 Islam Observed: Religious Development in Morocco and
    Indonesia. Chicago: University of Chicago Press.
  1973a The Impact of the Concept of Culture on the Concept of
    Man. *In* The Interpretation of Cultures. Clifford Geertz, ed.
    Pp. 33–54. New York: Basic Books.
  1973b Thick Description: Toward an Interpretive Theory of
    Culture. *In* The Interpretation of Cultures. Clifford Geertz,
    ed. Pp. 3–30. New York: Basic Books.

Goodenough, Ward H.
  1976 Multiculturalism as the Norman Human Experience.
  Anthropology and Education Quarterly 7(4):4–7.

Jackson, Phillip W.
  1968 Life in Classrooms. New York: Holt, Rinehart and Winston.

Kaler, Amy, and Melanie Beres
  2010 Essentials of Field Relationships. Walnut Creek, CA: Left
  Coast Press.

Keesing, Felix M.
  1958 Cultural Anthropology: The Science of Custom. New York:
  Rinehart and Company.

Kluckhohn, Clyde, and Henry A. Murray, eds.
  1948 Personality in Nature, Society, and Culture. New York:
  Alfred A. Knopf.

Kulick, Don, and Margaret Willson, eds.
  1995 Taboo: Sex, Identity and Erotic Subjectivity in
  Anthropological Fieldwork. London: Routledge.

Kutsche, Paul
  1998 Field Ethnography: A Manual for Doing Cultural
  Anthropology. Upper Saddle River, NJ: Prentice Hall.

Lave, Jean, and Etienne Wenger
  1991 Situated Learning: Legitimate Peripheral
  Participation. New York, NY: Cambridge University
  Press.

Lewin, Ellen, and William L. Leap
  1996 Out in the Field. Urbana: University of Illinois Press.
  2002 Out in Theory. Urbana: University of Illinois Press.

Macnair, Peter L.
  1986 From Kwakikutl to Kwakwa ka'wakw. *In* Native Peoples:
  The Canadian Experience. R. Bruce Morrison and C.
  Roderick Wilson. eds. Pp. 501–519. Toronto: McClelland
  and Stewart.

Marcus, George
  1998 Sticking with Ethnography through Thick and Thin. *In*
  Ethnography through Thick and Thin. G. Marcus, ed., Pp.
  231-253. Princeton, NJ: Princeton University Press.

Mead, Margaret
  1928 Coming of Age in Samoa. New York: William Morrow
    and Co.
  1953 National Character. *In* Anthropology Today, A. L. Kroeber,
    ed. Pp. 642–667. Chicago: University of Chicago Press.

Miles, Matthew B., and Huberman, A. Michael
  1984 Qualitative Data Analysis: A Sourcebook of New Methods.
    Beverly Hills, CA: Sage Publications.

Opler, Morris E.
  1945 Themes as Dynamic Forces in Culture. American Journal
    of Sociology 51(3):198– 206.
  1969 Apache Odyssey: A Journey Between Two Worlds. New
    York: Holt, Rinehart and Winston.

Rohner, Ronald P.
  1968 *Review of* A Kwakiutl Village and School by Harry F.
    Wolcott. American Anthropologist 70(3):654.

Roth, Wolff-Michael
  2004 Autobiography as Scientific Text: A Dialectical Approach to
    the Role of Experience. Review Essay of Sneaky Kid and Its
    Aftermath. Forum: Qualitative Social Research (electronic
    journal). 5(1), January.

Sanjek, Roger
  1990 Fieldnotes: The Makings of Anthropology. Ithaca, NY:
    Cornell University Press.
  1991 The Ethnographic Present. Man, The Journal of the Royal
    Anthropological Institute 26:609–628.
  1998 What Ethnographies Leave Out. XCP: Cross-Cultural
    Poetics, Volume 3, pp. 99–111.

Schensul, Jean J., and Margaret D. LeCompte, eds.
  1999 The Ethnographer's Toolkit. 7 volumes. Walnut Creek, CA:
    AltaMira Press.

Smith, Louis M.
  1978 An Evolving Logic of Participant Observation, Educational
    Ethnography and Other Case Studies. *In* Review of Research
    in Education 6, Pp. 16–377. Washington, DC: American
    Educational Research Association.

Spindler, George D., ed.
  1955 Education and Anthropology. Stanford, CA: Stanford
    University Press.

1963 Education and Culture—Anthropological Approaches.
New York: Holt, Rinehart and Winston.
1974 Education and Cultural Process: Toward an Anthropology
of Education. New York: Holt, Rinehart and Winston.

Tax, Sol
1973 Self and Society. *In* Reading in Education: A Broader View.
Malcolm P. Douglass, ed. Pp. 41–58. Columbus, OH: Charles
E. Merrill.

Wolcott, Harry F.
1964 A Kwakiutl Village and Its School. Unpublished dissertation. School of Education, Stanford University.
1967 A Kwakiutl Village and School. New York: Holt, Rinehart
and Winston.
1973 The Man in the Principal's Office: An Ethnography. New
York: Holt, Rinehart and Winston.
1974 The Elementary School Principal: Notes from a Field
Study. In Education and Cultural Process. George D.
Spindler, ed. Pp. 176–204. New York: Holt, Rinehart and
Winston.
1977 Teachers vs. Technocrats: An Educational Innovation in
Anthropological Perspective. Eugene: University of Oregon
Center for Educational Policy and Management.
1982 Mirrors, Models, and Monitors: Educator Adaptations
of the Ethnographic Innovation. In Doing the Ethnography
of Schooling: Educational Ethnography in Action. George
D. Spindler, ed. Pp. 68-95. New York: Holt, Rinehart and
Winston.
1983a Adequate Schools and Inadequate Education: The Life
History of a Sneaky Kid. Anthropology and Education
Quarterly 14 (1):3–32.
1983b A Malay Village that Progress Chose: Sungai Lui and
the Institute of Cultural Affairs. Human Organization 42(1):
72–81.
1987 On Ethnographic Intent. In Interpretive Ethnography
of Education: At Home and Abroad. George and Louise
Spindler, eds. Pp. 37–57. Hillsdale, NJ: Lawrence Erlbaum
Associates.
1989 Afterword, 1989, A Kwakiutl Village and School, 25
Years Later. [Postscript added to the Waveland printing of A
Kwakiutl Village and School.]

1994 Transforming Qualitative Data: Description, Analysis, and Interpretation. Thousand Oaks, CA: Sage.

1995 The Art of Fieldwork. Walnut Creek, CA: AltaMira Press. [Second edition published 2005.]

2001 Writing Up Qualitative Research. 2nd ed. Thousand Oaks, CA: Sage.

2002 Sneaky Kid and Its Aftermath: Ethics and Intimacy in Fieldwork. Walnut Creek, CA: AltaMira Press.

2003a A Kwakiutl Village and School. Updated edition. Walnut Creek, CA: AltaMira Press.

2003b The Man in the Principal's Office: An Ethnography. Updated edition. Walnut Creek, CA: AltaMira Press.

2003c A "Natural" Writer. Anthropology and Education Quarterly 34(3):324–338.

2003d Teachers versus Technocrats. Updated version. Walnut Creek, CA: AltaMira Press.

2004 The Ethnographic Autobiography. Auto/Biography 12(2): 93–106.

2009 Writing Up Qualitative Research. 3rd ed. Thousand Oaks, CA: Sage.

2010 Overdetermined Behavior, Unforeseen Consequences. Qualitative Inquiry 16(1):10–20.

Zelditch, Morris, Jr.

1962 Some Methodological Problems of Field Studies. American Journal of Sociology 67:566–567.

ACKNOWLEDGMENTS

I owe two huge debts of gratitude, one to my mentor and friend of the past fifty years, Professor George Spindler of Stanford University; the other to my peripatetic publisher Mitch Allen, who has wooed me along a trail leading from Sage Publications to AltaMira Press to Rowman and Littlefield Publishers, and finally, to his most recent adventure, Left Coast Press. George Spindler, affectionately called "Spin" by his students, got me started in ethnography and has always been supportive, as well as making sure I stayed on track. As my mentor and muse began winding down from a long and successful career as teacher, editor, and author, Mitch was there to urge me on.

I am indebted as well to numerous colleagues and students who played a part along the way, and particularly to Dr. Mark Wohl, who graciously offered once again to read a manuscript in rough form, to offer constructive commentary, and to inform me of what he felt I should have written instead. I also acknowledge the thoughtful efforts of Dr. Heewon Chang and other former students she invited to join in nominating me for the special Career Award from the International Center for Qualitative Inquiry presented to me in May 2010, for dedication and contributions to qualitative research, teaching, and practice. And I thank Norman Delue, my life partner of the past forty plus years, who has shared in many of the experiences described in these pages.

NAME INDEX

SUBJECT INDEX

ABOUT THE AUTHOR

Harry F. Wolcott joined anthropology to his career as educator while pursuing doctoral studies at Stanford University. Fieldwork for his dissertation was conducted among the Kwakiutl people in the Alert Bay region of British Columbia, Canada. The monograph resulting from that study was *A Kwakiutl Village and School*. He completed doctoral studies in 1964, the year a network of educational research and development (R&D) centers was established throughout the United States, and he accepted a position as a research associate in the new R&D Center for the Study of Educational Administration at the University of Oregon. He is still at Oregon, where he has served on the faculties of education and anthropology, helped to develop the field of "anthropology and education," and pursued interests in ethnographic research and culture acquisition. He is now professor emeritus in the Department of Anthropology.

Field research following his initial work has taken him as far afield as Zimbabwe, Malaysia, and Thailand (where he served two Fulbright assignments), and as close as an elementary school across town. Two major studies conducted under the auspices of the R&D Center are *The Man in the Principal's Office: An Ethnography* (1973) and *Teachers Vs. Technocrats: An Educational Innovation in Anthropological Perspective* (1977). Through the years he has been a visiting professor, guest speaker, consultant, or external examiner at other universities in North America and in various other parts of the world. In 1989 he was a recipient of the George and Louise Spindler award for his distinguished scholarly contributions to the field of educational anthropology.

He has devoted the past twenty years to writing what has become a quartet on field research: a book on qualitative research titled *The Art of Fieldwork*; a book focused more exclusively on ethnography, *Ethnography: A Way of Seeing*, revised in 2008; an edited collection of shorter pieces to illustrate the processes of description, analysis, and interpretation under the title *Transforming Qualitative Data*; and a monograph, *Writing Up Qualitative Research*, revised and expanded in a third edition (2009). *Sneaky Kid and Its Aftermath* is his most recent study. And here he offers *Ethnography Lessons,* to sum it all up.